Secrets
of a
Successful,
Tranquil
Life

BOOKS IN THE DEMERS BOOKS
HEALTH AND WELL-BEING SERIES

Norma Sawyers-Kurtz, *How to Cope with the Loss of Your Child: A Guide for Grieving Parents* (2010). ISBN: 978-0-9816002-5-3

John V. Wylie, *Diagnosing and Treating Mental Illness: A Guide for Physicians, Nurses, Patients and Their Families* (2010). ISBN: 978-0-9816002-6-0

Eric G. Stephan and R. Wayne Pace, *7 Secrets of a Successful, Tranquil Life: A Guide for People Who Want to Get Out of Hyperdrive* (2010). ISBN 978-0-9816002-7-7

Danny M. O'Dell, *Strength Training for People with Osteoporosis: The Danny O'Dell Method* (2010). ISBN: 978-0-9816002-8-4

OTHER BOOKS OF INTEREST FROM
DEMERS BOOKS AND MARQUETTE BOOKS

John Wheeler, *Last Man Out: Memoirs of the Last Associated Press Reporter Castro Kicked Out of Cuba in the 1960s* (2009). ISBN: 978-0-9816002-0-8

Tom Graves, *Crossroads: The Life and Afterlife of Blues Legend Robert Johnson* (2009). ISBN: 978-0-9816002-1-5

Charles J. Merrill, *Colom of Catalonia: Origins of Christopher Columbus Revealed* (2009). ISBN 978-0-9816002-2-2

John Schulz, Please Don't Do That! The Pocket Guide to Good Writing (2008). ISBN: 978-0-922993-87-1 (booklet)

Phillip J. Tichenor, *Athena's Forum: A Historical Novel* (2005). ISBN: 0-922993-27-0

Melvin DeFleur, *A Return to Innocence: A Novel* (2005). ISBN: 0-922993-50-5

David Demers, *China Girl: One Man's Adoption Story* (2004). ISBN: 0-922993-08-4

7 Secrets

of a Successful, Tranquil Life

A Guide for People Who Want to Get Out of Hyperdrive

Dr. Eric G. Stephan
Dr. R. Wayne Pace

Demers Books LLC • Spokane, Washington

Printed in the United States of America

Library of Congress Cataloging-in-Publication Data

2009906905

ISBN for this edition:

978-9816002-7-7

Cover Photo Courtesy of Fotolia.com

Demers Books LLC
3107 East 62nd Avenue
Spokane, Washington 99223
509-443-7057 (voice) / 509-448-2191 (fax)
books@demersbooks.com / www.DemersBooks.com

Dedication

To all the wonderful people who hop out of bed each morning with a determination to make it a great day, who have learned some of the secrets of being both successful and happy but want to learn more, and who find those rays of sunlight that brighten their lives and the lives of all with whom they come in contact. We thank you.

Table of Contents

Read This First!

W e wrote this book after talking to people in and out of our personal effectiveness seminars. We asked them if they were following the "ways," "techniques," and "methods" outlined in some of the most popular books in this market. Their response was always the same: "No!" They liked hearing or reading about the success stories of others and tried out a few ideas, but they felt many of the ideas were too unnatural and cumbersome to use in their own lives.

During some of our seminars, we teased the audiences with the idea that even though they had probably heard about the seven or eight habits of highly effective people, we were now going to teach them the "real secrets of successful and very happy people!" After considerable laughter and applause, we shared with them the ideas that we are now going to share with you in this book — ideas that have been gleaned from considerable research and study in the fields of success and happiness. The suggestions are practical, easy to use, and can generate a large return for a small investment of time. The best thing is that the approaches and ideas can be equally useful at work, home, and in one's personal life.

On one occasion, after sharing some of these ideas with a group of businessmen, several of them came up afterward and said, "You have got to share these suggestions with our wives." After we shared the ideas with a group of parents, many of them also told us, "I wish my teenage children were here. They run around like they have their heads on backwards. They need to hear this."

We now invite you to come with us as we take you through a series of seven important actions for improving your life. We call them "secrets" because, for some reason, they seem hidden to many people. From our past experience of sharing these ideas with literally thousands of people from all walks of life, we can make an important promise to you: If you will take the time to relax a little, read this book, and do what we ask you to do, you will enjoy one of the best experiences of your life. Not only will you enjoy a great experience applying simple ideas, but as one of our book endorsers, Dr. Stephen Covey, says, "You will become the creative force in your own life."

These seven secrets will help you:

(1) Untangle yourself from the infinite demands of daily living and help you focus on the most important things in your life;
(2) Find hidden resources you can use so that you can actually accomplish more by doing less;
(3) Be more creative in the way you approach tasks, problems, and concerns, so you can find easier and more effective solutions;
(4) Make time to pursue your own goals and aspirations or do nothing (you will love finding the time to do nothing);
(5) Strengthen yourself so you don't feel weary when the whole world tries to fall down on you;
(6) Discover a more calm and peaceful way to live as you increase your personal effectiveness; and

(7) Get your life moving ahead in a happier and more productive way.

As you proceed through these important ideas, what matters to you and what doesn't matter to you will become immediately evident. In other words, we want you to "stop swatting mosquitoes" and pay more attention to the "alligators." Actually, we will help you learn a few secrets that will free up your thinking and help you avoid "sweating" the big and the small stuff.

This book will help you look at the most intrusive things in your life that keep you from fully realizing the great potentials that you have. If you follow along carefully, you will be able to throw out some of the unnecessary "junk" in your life, implement a few simple and practical actions to make yourself more successful and to help you live your life in a calmer and happier manner.

You can do it. Thousands before you have done it. When you finish reading this section, go to Chapter 1, which contains the first action you must take to get yourself untangled from some of the unnecessary burdens of daily living. We call it "Shift Out of Hyperdrive."

With overflowing gratitude, we once again acknowledge the long-time and sustained support given to us by our spouses, Sandra Utley Stephan and Gae Tueller Pace, the two people who are usually underwhelmed by our endeavors, but who patiently, kindly, and lovingly suffer through our own brand of relaxed hyperactivity. They are our lifetime traveling companions who demonstrate endurance unknown even to their closest observers.

Dr. Eric G. Stephan, Orem, Utah
Dr. R. Wayne Pace, St. George, Utah

Shift Out of Hyperdrive

Are you feeling a little beat up? Do you sometimes feel like someone is turning you upside down and dropping you on your head? Do you sometimes feel frustrated and overwhelmed by all the things you are expected to do? Each of these feelings may be triggered by a variety of actions. Are you one of those people who tries to do more and more in less and less time? Or do you take on too many responsibilities, concerns and worries? Do you rush to achieve everything and feel guilty for completing nothing very well? Maybe you're the type of person who can't even relax at home without feeling restless.

It seems like everyone is trying to do more than they feel able to do. They seem determined to compete successfully with the whole world and do whatever it takes to be an ideal employee, an excellent mom, a great dad, a perfect neighbor, a gallant friend, a loving husband or wife, and an all around Good Samaritan to everyone. Even when you try to relax by reading a newspaper or watching a TV news program you are reminded that terrorism continues to be a threat to the United States, and that the once steady and rising stock market is acting like a yo-yo, layoffs are becoming more common place, and carefully crafted retirement plans are flying out the window left and right. Crime rates are up and people continue to treat each other in the most inhumane ways. No wonder you sometimes feel a little emotionally drained and perplexed. The whole world seems to be falling apart.

Why You Feel So Frustrated

You may be engaged in a chronic struggle with yourself, with others, with work, and with life itself. Maybe you're still stuck in the "activity trap" and haven't learned to take some time for yourself. One moment you feel proud because working harder than anyone else "proves" that you're worthwhile and an important person. The next moment you realize that you're just "spinning your wheels," unable to move in any direction.

Most likely you don't have much spare time. When you get too busy, the term "spare time" becomes an oxymoron. The words "spare" and "time" don't seem to belong next to one another. If spare time doesn't exist for you, it means you're "hyperliving." You're speeding along the surface of life, moving rapidly from task to task, completing one task so that you can begin the next one and failing to enjoy what you're doing. Plus, you're probably failing to take a minute to sit back, relax, and admire the task that you've just completed.

With hyperliving, you lose perspective. Relationships are ignored. Things of real value become lost in the daily urgencies of life. And often, the consequences of this quick-paced way of living are ulcers, heart attacks, irritability, and an inability to be tender and loving. If you are in a position of leadership in your organization, your followers will soon detect that you are losing hope in and enthusiasm for your job. They may feel that you don't have the time and energy to solve work problems effectively, to listen to their concerns, or to vigorously pursue lofty organizational goals and dreams. When this starts to happen, you become less effective as a leader. But the true sadness occurs when you keep yourself so frustrated and anxious that you're unable to really listen to the broken sentences of a little child, to notice the spring flowers beginning to bud, or to observe how clouds seem to turn their dark sides down before the warm summer rain begins. Would you like to know how well you're doing in terms of coping with the tumult and demands of everyday living?

Take This Quiz

Pause from your reading for just a minute and answer the following questions. Mark a "y" for yes or an "n" for no at the end of each question.

Do you:

_____ Wake up feeling a little overwhelmed and discouraged?
_____ Worry about how you are going to spend your day?
_____ Experience regular sleep problems, fatigue, headaches, or digestive difficulties?
_____ Fly off the handle or sulk when co-workers and family members don't do things right?
_____ Forget things?
_____ Have a hard time focusing on or finishing the task at hand?

_____ Find it hard to tell others that you are stressed out and need help with projects?

_____ Depend on increased use of medication or drugs to get through periods of frustration?

_____ Fall apart when someone criticizes something that you are doing?

_____ Feel discouraged or run-down at the end of the day?

The more "yes" answers you have, the more likely it is that you may not be dealing with the demands of daily living in the most efficient way.

You are not alone. We all feel frustrated and stressed from time to time. The most important questions include the following: Can you do better? Can you return to a more normal life, where you accomplish more by doing less? Can you find leisure time to pursue your own dreams while you are helping others? Can you really live life with more health and confidence, more focus and purpose, and with more peace and calm?

The answer to all of these questions is a resounding "YES!" You can change your life, and if you don't you might find life considerably shorter than you expect. Consider, for example, what Maggie Wilderotter, former CEO and President of Wink Communications, Inc., in Almaeda, Calif., did to avoid feeling overworked, overwhelmed and burned out.

I've never burned out on the job, simply because I don't let myself get to that point. You've got to be able to pace yourself and allow time for plenty of breaks. I have three golden rules: Weekends are for my family, not for my work; I take four weeks of vacation each year; and I try to maintain a healthy lifestyle — by sleeping enough, eating well and exercising often.

Maggie added that "Time is a finite resource, and we all place infinite demands on it. I view time as an opportunity, as a chance to make choices about how I spend that resource — because it is our choice. And that's something that people often forget."

Do you (1) pace yourself, (2) allow time for plenty of breaks during the day and to be with your family, and (3) maintain a healthy lifestyle? People who are starting to get caught up in a nonsatisfying style of living usually don't do any of these things consistently. Remember, time is a finite resource.

A Tremendous Whack!

Winston Churchill once said, "If you have an important point to make, don't try to be subtle or clever. Use a pile driver. Hit the point once. Then come back and hit it again. Then hit it a third time — a tremendous whack."

Let's follow Churchill's advice right now. Get ready for an insightful whack. Take a deep breath, relax, and read the following very slowly:

You can't do it all. You can't do it all. You can't do it all.

You will never have enough time to do all the things that you feel you should, maintain your own strength and energy, be with and strengthen your family, serve your neighbors, church, and community, advance in your profession, and pursue your own dreams.

Your deepest frustration comes when you're being told that you can do it all when you know that you really can't. Once you buy in to the "you can do it all myth," you begin to frustrate yourself and will continue to frustrate yourself for the rest of your life. Why? Because nobody in this whole world has enough time and energy to do all the things they feel that they should do or would like to do.

Can you imagine how many people are running around trying to do the impossible in a day? And how many people fall into bed at night clutching a list of things that they didn't get done today, but swear that they will get done tomorrow?

What about you? Do you drop into bed feeling like you're further behind than when the day started? Or do you find yourself having been busy all day, but without having accomplished the most important things you really wanted to do?

An article from *Executive Focus* magazine was recently forwarded to us by a friend who works in the publishing industry. The article was titled: "How Top Executives Manage to Do It All." The irony is that top executives simply can't do it all. In fact, former Disney CEO Michael Eisner refuses to work late if he's made a commitment to his children. Columbia TriStar Motion Pictures Vice Chairman Lucy Fisher works a four-day schedule and dedicates Fridays to her family. Telecommunications mogul John Malone works just five hours a day and yet takes the time to drive home for lunch.

All these people have enormous responsibilities but have simplified their lives and focused their efforts in such a way as to have time for "leisure, family, hobbies and other personal pursuits." If these people hadn't learned how to reorganize their work and life a little better, they would be in the same kind of turbulent living that you may be experiencing.

Something's Gotta Give

Unfortunately, when you become too involved with things to do, both on and off the job, the first thing that starts to give is your own emotional health, happiness, and well being. Remember, time is finite; there is only so much of it. Yet, the demands that everyone — including yourself — puts on their time are infinite. You can only do so much. You can't do it all. The biggest tragedy occurs when you don't use some of your time to sit down and smell the flowers, or watch the trees bend in the morning breeze, or think about how grateful you are to just be alive!

Start in the Right Direction

When you feel overloaded and frustrated by all the things that are going on in your life, don't compound your problems by feeling resentful, angry, and guilty. These are normal responses when you feel overwhelmed and frustrated by situations in which you find yourself. Don't for one second feel that there is something wrong with you. There isn't. On the contrary, treat these feelings as evidence that you're a sensitive and responsive human being. Be grateful for being perceptive and alive.

When you experience these negative feelings, prove that you have control over your life by acknowledging them and doing something about them. We all have extra baggage in our lives. It's what you do about that baggage that makes the difference between being happy and successful or continuing along with feelings of discouragement and despair.

You Can Do Something, But Not Everything

Imagine that you're in a personal effectiveness seminar. The speaker has a huge blackboard. Her first question to the 250-member audience is: "Do any of you work for a living?" After a bit of laughter from everyone, she asks: "What should you be doing to get ahead at work?"

A multitude of hands go flying into the air. People shout out numerous items:

"Figure out how to make my work simpler."

"Catch up on some overdue reports."

"Research a new project."

"Help a coworker understand his job."

"Repair a relationship with my boss."

"Cut costs."

"Be a better team player."

"Learn more about quality management procedures."

"Delegate more effectively."

"Get more feedback about how I am doing as a manager."

"Start networking because my job is in jeopardy."

The seminar speaker is writing on the board as quickly as she can. After a few minutes of frantically trying to keep up with all the answers to the first question, the speaker asks the audience a second question: "What are all the things that you feel you should be doing for your spouse and your family?" Dozens of hands go up and people shout out their thoughts:

"Take a vacation."

"Spend more time teaching my children about life."

"Get my spouse out of the house more often."

"Attend more of my children's sporting activities."

"Build a playhouse."

"Help my son with his math class."

"Set aside one night a week to be together as a family."

"Make recreation a family activity."

"Do a better job of dividing family member responsibilities."

"Figure out a better way of helping each other with individual tasks."

"Start having a weekly 'date night' with my spouse."

It becomes pretty obvious that everyone has a multitude of things that they feel they should be doing for their spouse and family.

The seminar speaker continues recording audience responses. After a short time the blackboard is covered with things that members of the audience feel that they should do at work and with their spouse and family. The speaker then asks an interesting third question: "What are all the things you feel you should be doing in your neighborhood, for your friends, and in your community and church?" Once again a sea of hands shoots into the air accompanied by new responses:

"Help more with community service projects."

"Give some blood to the blood bank."

"Help an ill neighbor."

"Contribute some time or resources to the poor."

"Help raise money for a charitable organization."

"Run for a local political office."

"Look after my neighbor who recently lost her husband."

"Join at least one community organization."

"Join the parent-teacher group."

"Be a pink-lady at the hospital."

"Fill my church assignment more consistently."

"Take responsibility for contributing to neighborhood security efforts."

"Organize a neighborhood get-acquainted progressive dinner."

The blackboard is now totally filled. An almost awkward silence fills the auditorium as everyone wonders where they go from here.

Then the speaker asks: "Is anyone here doing all of these things?" Heads shake sheepishly back and forth indicating a big "No." "Neither am I," says the speaker. "It is impossible to do everything you feel you should do at your place of employment, in your family, in the community, and in your neighborhood.

With an audible sigh of relief, the audience exhales and starts smiling again. The speaker doesn't seem too worried about not being able to do everything, so a temporary *why should I worry feeling* settles over the minds of the participants.

Now, imagine that the speaker concludes her inquiry by asking: "What things should you be doing for yourself, for your own health and well-being? Do you have a leisure-time activity — a hobby — that gives you pleasure and a break from everything else in life? Do you take time to sit and do nothing once in awhile? Do you attend to your own personal needs, or do you neglect them because you're taking care of everyone and everything else? Are you taking time to work on your own personal goals and dreams?" This time the silence is deafening!

Most people find themselves fitting rather well into the above scenario: trying to do it all and not taking sufficient time for themselves. On your deathbed, will you wish that you had spent more time at work? If your answer is a definite "No," then what do you wish you had spent more time doing? You might resolve the dilemma by understanding that you can only devote your time and energy to a few things. If you have a job or career, that is one thing. If you have a family, that's another thing, and that may leave you with only a few more areas to which you can devote time and energy. You can make an effort to do volunteer work in your community, join a neighborhood organization, or engage in a regular fitness or recreational activity program.

Most people understand intuitively that they can only do so many things, but they keep overcommitting themselves and overcomplicating their lives anyway. To begin to restore some semblance of sanity to your life, you must figure out what your most important personal concerns and priorities are, and then say "no" to everything else.

In a recent popular book about being an organized executive, a topic covered was, "How to juggle multiple priorities." Our recommendation to you, whether or not you are an executive, is simply this: Stop Juggling! Married or not, parent or not, stop rushing around trying to overextend your self at home, at work, and in the community. Start small. Drop one of the many items you're trying to keep afloat. If you can, let someone else do it. If not, then just learn to say "no" and move on to those things that may be more significant to you.

Restoring Sanity: A Model

To get off the merry-go-round kind of life that leads to unhealthy amounts of discomfort and distress, you'll need an easy-to-follow,

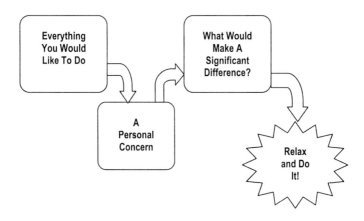

practical plan. You'll need an approach that responds to the fact that you can't do it all.

Our Super Sanity Model provides a simple strategy that allows you to start digging yourself out from under a lot of demands that are placed upon you. The plan allows you to leverage opportunities that surround you.

Notice the first rectangle in the model on the left labeled: "Everything you would like to do." This rectangle encompasses everything you would like to do or feel you should be doing at work, home, in the community, and for yourself, but can't do because there are only 24 hours in a day and you don't have an infinite supply of time.

The second rectangle is labeled: "A personal concern." Here is where you make some initial decisions about what you can do and what you should focus on. Your biggest gains in dumping that frenetic feeling and regaining control of your life come when you identify a few important personal concerns and make them your top priority. For example, if you find yourself worrying and stewing about a problem at work, or over a member of your family, write it down as a personal concern.

What else do you regularly think about that creates a great personal concern? To help you identify your concerns, grab a pencil and respond to each of the following questions. You won't be able to resolve a concern if you leave it in a general or vague form. Be specific. In fact, the more specific the concern, the easier it is to resolve.

1. My biggest concern at work is

2. My most significant family or spouse concern is

3. Right now my major financial concern is

4. During a typical day I think most about how I'm going to

5. I feel most uncomfortable about my personal growth when

6. On my deathbed, I will wish that I had spent more time

7. If I could do anything that I wanted to do, I would probably

Did these questions lead you to write down a few personal concerns? If there are other things in your life that weigh heavily on your mind each day, write those down now:

8. Other things that weight you down include

Now go back and look at your list of personal concerns. Pick out three or four that are the most bothersome. Don't worry about everything on your list. You can take care of other items later. The most important thing is to get the heaviest monkeys off your back and the most troublesome things out of your mind.

The third rectangle in the model asks you to consider carefully each of your initial three or four concerns and to decide what you can do about each concern that would make a significant difference in resolving that concern. The emphasis here is on significant difference. Don't focus on effort. Focus on results. Is there something you can do to take care of the concern once and for all? Try to fire the rifle instead of the shotgun. If you can possibly avoid it, don't put a temporary patch on a problem and hope that it will go away. Find a solution and a course of action that will resolve your concern once and for all.

In a report in *Fast Company* magazine, Bix Norman, executive vice president of Manufacturing and Information Technology at Herman Miller Inc., says, "I never worry about burnout, because I manage my schedule so that I never get drained." Now here is the important point: "I make sure that I focus only on what's important. I'll pick three aspects of a particular project to give my attention to. Luckily, I've been good at identifying the few things that make a big difference."

With each of the three or four personal concerns that you've highlighted, decide what you can do that makes a significant difference in resolving that concern. Don't be timid in your thinking and don't be restricted in your approach to ridding yourself of a personal concern.

A Concern and a Significant Action at Work

Whether at home or work, the process of focusing on a specific concern and doing something that will make a significant difference in resolving that concern is an extremely vital step in taking care of a problem. In the following situation we were trying to help some managers get out from under a few concerns that seemed to be taking an inordinate amount of their time. A manager of a local software company said that his biggest concern was an employee who simply wasn't carrying his share of the load. This employee was a personal friend of the manager. They were neighbors and had known each other for a long time. The manager felt obligated to keep him in the company.

In this case, we thought we would help the manager arrive at an action that would make a significant difference with his concern. We asked the manager, "Does the employee have a problem that can be fixed with a little training?" The answer was "no." "Have you tried to motivate this employee with additional rewards and by increasing his involvement in the work?" The manager's answer was "yes." "Have you looked for another place in the company where this employee may be more interested in the work and his co-workers?" "Yes" was the manager's response. "Have you given the employee fair warning about what will happen to him if things don't change, and have you given him more than one opportunity to make some changes in his work and attitude?" Again the manager's response was "yes, we have been all through that on more than one occasion."

There is a saying in business and industry that goes like this: "Reward or replace." This simply means that if people can't be rewarded for their work and you've tried all the possibilities mentioned above, then you simply quit stalling and replace the person. That was our response: "Replace the person. You'll do yourself a favor and at the same time you'll probably be doing the employee a favor, even if he is your best friend."

Something obviously was quite wrong in this situation. The employee was not responding to opportunities to make things better, and the manager and the employee needed to get on with their respective lives. For both to sit there in a state of denial and paralysis was a fairly useless consumption of time. Something significant needed to be done. Firing the employee was the best course of action to resolve this concern.

A Significant Difference in the Family

During one of our workshops designed especially for women, we were discussing the idea of doing significant things about a concern that was bugging them. A mother of several children mentioned that she was overloaded with doing things for her children. Several of her children were between 9 and 15 years of age. Among other things she mentioned the burden of trying to wash and iron their clothes, and constantly telling them to keep their rooms straight and less cluttered. She had barely mentioned what she was experiencing when several other mothers raised their hands and said they had similar problems with their children.

We decided to have a "fire the rifle" brainstorming session. These mothers, acting with each other's support, were definitely not timid in their approach to ridding themselves of unnecessary concerns. One mother said that she was going to teach her children how to do their own washing and ironing. She stated quite clearly that "she was sick and tired of doing things that the kids could do for themselves."

Another mother said that she had pleaded and begged her son to pick up after himself and to keep his room from looking like a nuclear device had recently been detonated in it. She wearily said that she just didn't know what to do anymore. In response, another understanding mother suggested that if the son refused to take a minute to make his bed and keep things straight, that she should "start removing furniture from the room, starting with the bed and TV!" These initial suggestions opened a floodgate of other specific ideas to help take care of concerns about children.

The whole idea is to focus on results. What can you do that will make a significant difference in the concern that you are facing. If you can't figure out a useful approach by yourself, ask friends, neighbors, or co-workers about their experiences with a similar problem.

Every problem and concern is solvable. You need to stop worrying about everyone and everything. Take a few concerns at a time and solve them. Don't make a feeble effort to take care of a concern. Figure out how to make a significant difference so that you don't keep thinking about the problem over and over again. If you can't figure out what to do with a concern, don't spend a lot of time fussing and stewing about it, ask someone who has dealt with a similar situation before. They may suggest a specific action that you could take to resolve your own concern.

If you have major financial, health, emotional, or relational concerns, go to a professional and get some help. Don't keep dwelling on the concerns. Get some knowledge about the concern. Then, based on that newly acquired knowledge, make a decision. Spring into action and change something for the better.

Relax and Do It

After you've decided that you can't do everything that you would like to at your place of work, in your family, for your community, and for your friends and neighbors, and you have decided what would make a significant difference with an important personal concern, then relax and do it. Don't get all up tight and nervous. You've thought about what you're going to do to take care of the concern. You've sought out special ideas and information on the subject. This is the moment to implement your idea.

Relax. Take a few deep breaths and visualize yourself moving forward with your plan. See in your mind's eye being peaceful and comfortable as you make the change. Feel the great relief that occurs as you resolve this one personal concern. This is the payoff for deciding how to make a significant difference with one of your personal concerns. Don't stop now and miss out on all the rewards of putting your idea into action.

Most of the time, you will find out that your worries about changing something in your life are unfounded. In the cases mentioned previously, the manager's friend was startled when he was let go from the organization. But the manager still maintained his friendship with the dismissed employee and reported to us that the employee said that he knew getting laid off was coming and that he learned a great lesson from it. Incidentally, the fired employee found a new job that suited him better and he was excited about his new found opportunity. The children of the mothers who were confronted with "no beds or TV" adjusted their behaviors rather quickly!

Albert Einstein once said, "The mere formulation of a problem is often far more essential than its solution." He suggested that once people decide what the specific concern is, the solution might be merely a matter of taking a rather obvious course of action.

Failure to Recognize a Concern at Work

In our work as organizational consultants, we've discovered that in the workplace, many people devote long hours to their jobs and assume that the workplace has a "norm" about working long hours when it really doesn't. A kind of company-wide ignorance develops because few employees want to talk about their concerns and struggles. Employees tend to think that everyone else is doing fine and that they are the only ones struggling.

We recently surveyed a major company in the hotel industry. The work expectations and the hours were horrendous. Apparently everyone thought that this was the norm or the culture of this particular company. When we came in as a neutral third party, the employees started to unfold their extreme discomfort with the long hours and unrealistic goals. We not only listened to their complaints and concerns, but we asked them for their recommendations and solutions to the problem. They had some pretty good ideas. They just needed someone to listen and carry their message upward in the chain of command in their organization. We did just that, and top management was surprised at the perceived company norm. Employees' perceptions, recommendations, and solutions helped the general managers make some useful changes with regard to the hours and work load of employees in that particular company.

You have to act. You must make necessary changes. You have to try; otherwise you'll find yourself in the same mess tomorrow as you are in today.

Making a Significant Difference at Home

After we had finished one of our seminars, several parents approached us and said, "My children rush from home to school and then on to a myriad of activities like they had their heads cut off." Every parent knows that a multitude of children's activities can turn a household into a three-ring circus.

Yes, children do need to engage in extracurricular activities. We all know the benefits. However, with dad working full time and mom trying to work part time, chauffeuring children and attending various activities can lead to feelings of overload and stress.

Frequently parents and children know that they are over committed, but they don't know how to remedy the situation. If ever there is a right time to sit down together and talk, this is it. You already know that no one can do all the things that he or she would like to do. No one has enough time or energy to do everything. So sit down with your family and decide what has to go.

Start by making a list of all the activities, times, dates, and places where family members are involved. This list might startle you and your children. Everyone may find that they are a little over-scheduled, especially when you realize that there isn't much time left over to wind down and relax. There may not be much free time for each child to be alone, read a book, or listen to some music.

You may also find out that the most important time of all may not exist: time with you. No activity can replace the interaction between you and your children. That's the time when both children and parents feel loved and important. That is the time when children acquire emotional security.

After you've made a list of all the scheduled activities of everyone, analyze each activity. Find out what's most important to each child. Then, keep the most significant ones and toss out the others. Help your children choose wisely so that they have time to celebrate their successes and time to be with you. Keep the lines of communication open with your spouse and children. This is a vital and ongoing activity. But if it is done well, everyone ends up a winner.

Taste the Sunshine

During one of our seminars, we asked the participants what they had learned so far in their instruction. Everyone had a great laugh when one middle-aged woman said that she felt she "was still hopelessly behind, but loving every minute of her progress." She had learned to relax and enjoy herself as she began to apply the suggestions made in the seminar.

If you've followed along carefully and tried out the suggestions that we've made, you've started to make a small but significant change in your life. By now you may realize that you can't do everything that you'd like to do for yourself, your family, your community, your neighbors, and at your place of employment. You've learned, however, to identify a few main concerns that keep worrying you, and you've figured out how to eliminate one or more of those concerns by focusing on results instead of effort.

You should have also experienced the peace and serenity that comes from taking short breaks. By the way, if you haven't taken a mini-break since starting your reading, why don't you do it right now. Go for a short walk, wander through a flower garden, or take a warm bath. If you can't do any of those, just get up and grab a drink of water, but be sure to drink slowly and taste the water. Taking breaks is one way to temporarily alleviate the stress and frustration that settles in when you feel a little anxious about the way you are living your life. After the break, take a few slow easy breaths and get going again. Read some more or act upon what you have already learned. Wallowing around in a puddle of self-pity and blaming others for your plight is useless. Instead, follow the advice of Ralph Waldo Emerson:

> Our strengths grow out of our weaknesses.
> Not until we are pricked and stung and sorely
> shot at, do we awaken the indignation which
> arms itself with secret forces.

Try Some Fly-Fishing!

This is no joke. Even if you are successful in writing down a few major concerns and doing something significant to resolve them and even though you are taking regular breaks and starting to throw off all your unwelcome burdens, life can still be tedious and frustrating. You need to have a hobby or engage in some leisure activity to distract you from some of the anxieties of everyday living.

An article in *USA Today*, dated Friday, June 21, 2002, pointed out that Charles Schwab fly-fishes, as does Martha Stewart, Bill Ford of Ford Motor, Meg Whitman of eBay, Time Warner's Ted Turner, Phil Satre of Harrah's Entertainment, Timberland's Jeffrey Swartz, and a host of other CEOs and retired CEOs. Why do they go fly-fishing? Their comments are all similar: Fly-fishing is "non-competitive and far removed from business"; "You learn to cope with rejection"; "The level of concentration allows you to abandon all thoughts about self"; and "It forces me to slow down."

Several of our friends who are leaders in their organizations learned how to fly airplanes during past military conflicts. Now, at least once a week, they find a plane they can rent and fly over the beautiful Rocky Mountains for about an hour or two just to "rise above the world and relax and enjoy life." Many people make a hobby out of recreational jogging, biking, and walking. Others turn to collecting, researching, writing, and other fun and relaxing activities. The secret here is to find something that interests you and takes your mind off "all thoughts about yourself." And, of course, do it regularly. Hit and miss, now and then, may only add to your frustrations of not being able to cope with life or even achieve a little mastery of a hobby.

Who has time for a hobby? Or who has time for a little regular recreation? You better have. If you don't, you're still in square one where spare time is an oxymoron and where you are still overwhelmed because you haven't yet learned that you can't do it all. This is a good way to benchmark your progress: Have you created a little time for yourself or for yourself and your spouse?

Comforting Thoughts for the Overwhelmed

From reading this chapter you've discovered that the first secret of success and happiness is for you to shift out of hyperdrive and stop trying to do everything. You can't do it all. Once that realization starts to sink in, you must be quick to learn how to throw off less essential activities and focus primarily on a few important personal concerns. If you don't learn how to do this, daily activities will crowd out high leverage opportunities. You may find yourself busy all day but without having successfully resolved those pesky problems that worry you or not having time to achieve significant goals in your life.

While you practice shifting out of hyperdrive, you can benefit from a few powerful thoughts to help keep you on track and encourage you to move ahead more quickly. Here are eight ideas to stimulate your thinking:

- Many of the problems that bother you now can go away. The dark clouds can pass. The sun can rise. As long as you are learning and doing something good, you're making progress, you're healing, and you're going to be fine.

- If you really get frustrated, don't yell at people or do anything self-destructive. Instead, go to the nearest pond and throw rocks into the water, or run down to the nearest zoo and scream your lungs out at the lizards.

- Don't blame others for your problems and don't have a long pity party. Remember, you — not others — are responsible for how you feel.

- While you're in a bit of frenzy, stay away from friends who are also stressing out. And don't use booze and drugs to find personal nirvana unless you want to end up on the short end of an "idiot-trip."

- Count some of the good things in your life. Breathe deeply. Surround yourself with positive messages. Breathe deeply. Play some great music. Breathe deeply. And by all means, LIGHTEN UP. (And don't forget to breathe deeply.)

- Have a bowl of real chicken soup — the kind your mother or grandmother used to make. If you can arrange it, have a delicious hot meal with your family and feel the strength of each member of the family.

- Realize that you are spiritual as well as physical. Learn to trust your inner conscience. If you need to, reconnect with your faith and see if you can find more of the inner peace that you've been looking for.

- Take control of your life. Take charge of yourself. The more you stop doing what doesn't work and start doing what does work, the faster you will achieve a sense of "Wow, I had no idea life could be this great!"

These eight thoughts should be reviewed each day. You may want to write them down and stick them on your mirror so that you can see them first thing in the morning. Thinking positive thoughts literally creates chemical entities within us. Two of these entities are hormones and neurotransmitters. Thinking positive thoughts gives us feelings of well-being.

In addition to reviewing these positive affirmations each morning, also look around and count a few of the good things in your life before you start your day. You will be surprised at how the day takes on a golden hue and things go better when you start the day with positive thoughts.

What to Do Next

Before you go to the next chapter, put this book down and relax for a minute. See what ideas from this first chapter still stick in your mind. If something does stick in your mind, it is probably because you've hit on an idea that works for you in resolving some of the frustrations in your life. Write that idea down on a piece of paper and act on it as quickly as possible.

After you have taken a little mental review of this chapter, flip back through the pages of this first chapter and notice all the ways to simplify your life and move ahead on the road to success and happiness. Especially, review the process of moving from all the things that you would like to do to singling out a few personal concerns. Make an effort this week to work on a personal concern. See if you can resolve it in such a way that you don't continue to worry about it every day.

One final thing before you go on to the next chapter. Take a relaxing mini-break. See if you can disconnect yourself for a few minutes from all the cares and concerns of the world. Have a little treat or just look up at the trees and the sky and be grateful that you are alive!

Whistle for Another Lever

A critical part of digging out from under some of your stresses and strains is identifying and learning how to use both your intrinsic and extrinsic resources. Many of the difficulties you are experiencing stem from the fact that you don't use your capabilities and resources very well.

You are surrounded by people who know how to do things better than you. They have knowledge and experience about many things you don't. On top of that, you may sometimes think that you have to do everything yourself, which leads to overlooking the numerous possibilities for help and support around you.

The first chapter was designed (1) to dispel the myth that you can do it all and (2) to encourage you to shift out of hyperdrive. This chapter seeks to remind you that you don't need to know how to do everything yourself to be successful, and you don't have to do everything yourself. You have all kinds of unused potential and resources that can help you achieve your goals and eliminate some of your problems. Let's begin with an interesting point of view captured in a story from the Far East.

An Eastern Parable

A wise martial arts master was ready to pass the mantle of authority for his organization to his No. 1 student. The master prepared a final test. He asked the student to move a large granite rock from one location to another before sunset. He told the student to use all of his power to accomplish the feat.

The student tried and tried but couldn't budge the rock. Just as he was about to give up, the master said, "Use all your power. Have you considered using a lever?"

"I didn't know I could use a lever," the student responded.

The student hurried and found a strong pole and began moving the rock. However, time was running out and he realized he couldn't accomplish the feat in time. In despair he sat down. The master quietly asked, "Have you used all of your power?"

The student cried, "Yes, I'm physically drained, mentally perplexed, and spiritually empty. I have no more power."

"Oh no," said the master, "you have more power than that."

The student looked up at the smiling master and sighed, "Where?"

The master smiled. "Right here," he said, pointing to himself. "Did you ask for my help? You have the power to ask for my help. Use all your power."

"Will you help me?" the humbled student asked.

"Yes," said the master.

Then, retrieving a golden whistle from his tunic, he signaled his other students, who had been hiding in the hills, to join them. They quickly moved the rock.

The moral of this story is that people don't use all of their power until they learn how to whistle for another lever.

People Are Your No. 1 Resource

You are surrounded by people and you have much knowledge available that can help you develop a successful strategy for achieving your goals. Consider your friends, teachers, family members, business associates, and neighbors, as well as the Internet, books, instruction manuals, and the city library as resources. Begin now to develop the mindset that everything and everyone is a resource. You are not alone. You simplify your life by using all your resources to find easier ways to do things. Asking questions and listening to answers is a simple way of plotting your way through life's frustrating dilemmas.

The key here is to treat everyone as a friend so that they are willing to help you accomplish a goal or provide insight that will answer a question. Don't vent your frustrations on your friends. They will not be impressed with your inability to cope. And don't scream at your relatives. They may scream back, accomplishing nothing. Remember the suggestion made in the first chapter, "If you have to scream, go to the zoo and scream at the lizards." They probably won't care what you're yelling about since they haven't studied much about contemporary abnormal psychology.

Let's pause on this topic for a moment. You have enough problems and frustrations without creating more for yourself. Undermining people by saying negative things about them and ignoring them, are all surefire ways to make enemies. Enemies are not likely to support you or help you. The last thing you need is to spend time worrying about who is your friend and who is your enemy. The critical question for you is this: Who will help you and give you good advice? You don't have time to worry about who is or isn't a friend. As Dale Carnegie says, "You can make more friends in two months by becoming interested in other people than you can in two years by trying to get other people interested in you."

Treating others as friends is such an easy and profitable thing to do. In fact, you already know how to do it because you have been treating certain people in your life as friends for many years.

Try this little experiment. Think of a good friend. Now imagine that you and your good friend have been separated a few weeks. Your friend went on a vacation and you haven't seen or talked to each other for three weeks. You walk down a hallway, look up, and see your friend coming toward you in the opposite direction. Try to imagine in your mind's eye, or even close your eyes and see, what you do as you and your friend meet in the hallway. Are you excited about seeing your friend? Do you smile? Do you hug? Do you say something? Do you make plans to go to lunch or talk longer later? Are you anxious to find out what your friend has been doing?

We all know how we treat our best friends. The challenge is to treat everyone as a good friend: smile, talk to them, listen to their ideas, give suggestions once in awhile, and be sure to make a little fuss over their achievements. They will like you. They will count you as one of their friends.

We all need to do more of this friendshiping in our own families. Notice how children spend hours talking to their friends, sharing dreams with them, defending them and helping them when they are in trouble or sad. Parents need to downplay their roles as parents and increase their roles as their children's best friends. Husbands and wives might benefit from giving up on trying to be the perfect husband and the perfect wife and go back to courting each other again and simply becoming each other's best friend.

This is a simple idea for using all your power and connecting better with the people around you. Consider treating your boss as a friend. Don't fight the boss. Help him or her. Smile, talk, ask questions, listen to directions, and praise the boss, and once in a while, share dreams and goals with him or her. Life with the boss is much easier and rewarding when you treat the boss as you treat one of your good friends. Start now to make everyone your friend by treating them as friends. It's easy, and you already know how to do it. A wise sage said that the time to make friends is before you need them.

The Success Triangle

We presented a seminar on how to be more successful and happy in Reno, Nevada. The seminar participants seemed particularly receptive to the ideas presented to them. A couple of days after we returned home, we received a letter in the mail. The letter, written by one of the organizers and participants, expressed appreciation for the many useful ideas presented at the seminar. He stated that he could immediately implement the ideas in his family, work, and community life. He was anxious to teach his family and coworkers what he had learned in the seminar about handling the challenges of every day living a little better and becoming a more effective and successful person.

He explained that the most useful concept that he had learned was called "The Success Triangle." He called it the "success hypothesis," because he felt as though this one principle could contribute more to an individual's personal success than anything else he had heard. If you don't learn much else from this book, pay careful attention to this concept. The Success Triangle (see figure)

The Success Triangle

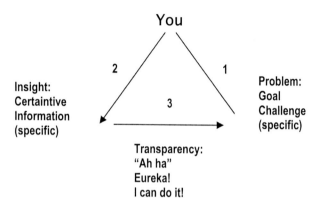

is a way to think about accomplishing tasks, solving problems, and getting things done while minimizing failure. To begin, put yourself at the top of the triangle.

Step 1

Go down the right side of the triangle and decide what it is that you want to do. Write down one challenging thing that you would like to accomplish, such as buying a house, writing a book, overhauling your family's poor nutritional eating habits, improving your financial situation, changing the behavior of an extremely difficult child, or starting a popular Chinese fast-food restaurant.

Step 2

Go down the left side of the triangle to "Certaintive Information." This means that you are going to ask three or four people, who have successfully done what you would like to do, how they did it. This is a good argument for treating others as friends. People tend to be more helpful when they work with friends. However, don't ask people who have no experience with what you are trying to accomplish even if you treat them as friends. Be selective. Personal friends and relatives are not good candidates for certaintive information unless they have been successful at doing what ever it is that you want to do.

Successful people are willing to share their success knowledge if you are sincere and in need of their experience. Pick out three people who have done what you are trying to do, or something quite similar to what you are trying to do, and be prepared to ask them specific questions that will enable you to accomplish your goal.

Incidentally, this procedure is not unlike a strategy used by several Asian countries when investigating the possibility of starting an automobile company in their country. Representatives from the country visit several of the best automobile manufacturing facilities in the world. They ask specific questions about everything from production and marketing to financing. They inquire about the strengths and weaknesses of the company. They ask what should be done differently if the company organizers were to do it all over again. After visiting several automotive companies, it is no Herculean task to design a car company better than any that they visited. The investigators throw out the weaknesses found in each manufacturing facility. They engineer using the best procedures possible. Suddenly, lo and behold, a car company better than all the rest emerges.

This is exactly what happens when you use step two. You should ask specific questions that give you the information and confidence to go ahead and accomplish your own project. Also, this step reduces the chances of failure. In other words, the more sound, accurate, and certaintive information you receive, the more you eliminate the possibility of something going wrong when you move ahead on your own idea.

By the way, small businesses often overlook Step 2. We had offices next door to a small business center. This gave us an opportunity to inquire about how the center was trying to help people with their businesses. The leader of the center told us that about 80 percent of the small businesses that he became acquainted with failed during the first year. We asked why? The answer was that the would-be business owners didn't learn enough about production, financing, marketing, or even selecting a good location for their businesses before they started them. They had been too carried away with the emotion of becoming a business owner and seeing their name in lights. Clearly, they had overlooked Step 2 in the success triangle. They needed more certaintive information, not advice from friends and others who had never been in business, about what it was like to "have to meet payroll" and pay the numerous other costs associated with doing business.

The saddest part of the small business center story was that people came to the center for help when it was too late. Instead of getting good information on how to proceed before they started putting together their business, they came after they were failing and had already mortgaged their homes to keep afloat. It was sad. But most of it could have been avoided by placing a higher priority on obtaining the experienced insight of others who were already succeeding in business. Too many of these people had failed to whistle for another lever. As Charles P. Steinmetz put it, "No man really becomes a fool until he stops asking questions."

Our suggestion is to avoid a heavy investment of time and money until you have completed this second step. You must reduce your probability of failure. In a sense, you can be successful at everything you do if you have the sound experience of others who have succeeded before you. Personally, we would not try to do much of anything significant without first obtaining as much practical knowledge as we can about how to proceed.

We have asked literally thousands of seminar participants, "What is the easiest, quickest way to find out how to do something successfully?" After a few responses, which usually include reading a book on the subject, someone always hits on the idea of asking a person who has done it successfully. It's amazing. Once that answer is vocalized, everyone immediately joins in a chorus: "Yes, that's it. That's the quickest and easiest way for learning how to do something successfully." Heed the slogan from Total Quality Management: "Measure twice, cut once. Do it right the first time."

Step 3

This step always occurs, but at a different time for each of us. As you obtain good information about how to do something successfully, a moment comes when you know you know how to do it. Sometimes that moment is call the "ah hah" experience. Others call it a "eureka experience." Still others call it a moment of "transparency." This is a great moment. It's an exciting time. You will feel the rush and the assurance that you know how to proceed in a successful manner.

This insight of knowing how to proceed may come at different times for each of us. The reason is that we all have a different set of experiences and a unique knowledge base upon which we build.

If you have experience writing articles, a small amount of certaintive information from successful writers may be all you need to proceed to write your own book. Someone else who has not written extensively about anything may need more information and support before feeling confident enough to proceed. If you don't have this feeling, you may want to gather more information about how others have proceeded successfully.

Anyone can rush into failure. You are planning to succeed. Take your time, but when you have done your homework, relax and do something to initiate your project or plan. Nothing much happens if you keep patting yourself on the back for coming up with a brilliant idea and then fail to do anything about implementing it.

Listen to These Success Stories

Several college age students decided to use the success triangle. Each, however, had a different goal that they wanted to achieve. One wanted to buy an apartment house for students. Another wanted to publish a book. And a third wanted to expand his father's multimillion-dollar business.

We instructed them to be as specific as possible about the goal they wanted to achieve. How large of an apartment house do you want to buy? What kind of book do you want to publish? And, in what way do you want to expand your father's business? The more specific the goal, the easier it is to achieve it. Ambiguous goals are not only hard to achieve, but impossible to obtain specific information about how to achieve them.

Then we instructed each of them to go to at least three people who had achieved success in the area in which they were interested. For the apartment house buyer, it meant that he needed to find three people who had purchased apartment houses and were running them profitably. The book author needed to go to three or more authors who had published successfully in her topical area and ask each of them how they got published. The young man who wanted to expand his father's business needed to find several people who had expanded into that area of endeavor and ask them how they did it and what problems to watch out for. Each of these people had an amazing experience as they used the success triangle model.

Buying a Student Apartment

The apartment buyer found out that student rentals were moving from one part of town to another, and that parking, plumbing, and depreciation were huge concerns in purchasing an apartment unit that would be profitable. He also discovered that once you decide on a price range and an area, you could get a real estate company to find all the possible options for you. This particular young man then persuaded one of the successful student apartment owners to accompany him in looking at the units that were available. The owner made numerous observations about what was good and what was not so good about each unit. Finally, the student asked the successful owner to make a recommendation as to which unit he would purchase. Acting upon a terrific amount of useful information and the recommendation of a successful owner, the student purchased a student apartment unit. His unit is profitable at the present time.

Writing a Book

The young lady who wanted to publish a book was able to ask several authors who had published successfully in her area of interest how they did it. She prepared a set of specific questions (a splendid idea) that she wanted to ask each author: What style of writing works best for this kind of book? Do I need a coauthor who has already published? Which publishing companies seem most interested in this topic? Do I query first or write the manuscript first? Which editors do you know who might be interested in accepting a manuscript? To whom would I take my query? Would you like to edit and coauthor my book? Is it best to find an agent?

By the way, this student wanted to publish a book for women. She also wanted the book to have a religious flavor to it. So she called and talked to authors who had specifically written about women and had taken a Christian approach. She even learned about using biblical references and other appropriate illustrations. After a few months of blood, sweat, and tears, she too was successful in achieving her goal.

Expand a Business

The graduating student who wanted to increase and expand his father's business was also successful. He decided, after receiving a lot of information about adding new products to his father's business, to add a healthier organic potato to the family potato business. He asked others who had done it successfully what to avoid and what to do to produce a bumper crop. He learned that they could sell their organic potatoes for a much better profit than their nonorganic potatoes. In the process of asking about expanding his father's business, the student also found out that imperfect and nonsalable potatoes could be made into "instant potatoes" and sold very profitably. He asked enough questions about how to process these nonsalable potatoes until he was certain that he could do it successfully. And he did, to the tune of tens of thousands of dollars!

In each case, these students, by proceeding carefully and following the success triangle, avoided the failure that so often accompanies efforts to be successful in accomplishing something worthwhile. Many who have used the success triangle formula still can't believe how simply successful they have been, whether trying to be an entrepreneur in the world of commerce or being successful at home.

A Style of Interaction for Maximizing Levers

To implement The Success Triangle effectively, you must interact positively with others, take the initiative, and move ahead when you have enough information to pursue a goal successfully. This is a good time to find out how you interact with others. We call the pattern of interacting with others your "operating style." Your style can be described and measured to give you a clearer idea about how you work with others to achieve your goals.

Operating Styles Profile

Complete the Operating Styles Profile (see next page), an instrument that uses metaphors to holistically characterize the way you interact with others. It's extraordinarily accurate and takes only a few minutes to complete. Scoring procedures allow you to identify a primary operating style and calculate how strongly your actions convey that style.

Metaphors can be useful. For example, we all think of Mohammed Ali when he described his boxing style as "Float like a butterfly, sting like a bee." Do you interact with others like a trumpet or a violin? Circle the one term in each group that characterizes, in metaphorical form, the way in which you interact or work with others.

a. Tiger	a. Steel Cable	a. Chain saw
b. Fox	b. Rope	b. Shears
c. Owl	c. Scaffold	c. Box
d. Lamb	d. Slipper	d. Carpet
a. Sand Blaster	a. Jack Hammer	a. Boom Box
b. Brillo Pad	b. The Sun	b. Polo Pony
c. Bucket	c. Filing Cabinet	c. Dugout
d. Facial Tissue	d. Letter	d. Kitten
a. Football Player	a. Freeway	a. Dynamite
b. Card Player	b. Interchange	b. Silk Tie
c. Chess Player	c. Stroll	c. Clock
d. Croquet Player	d. Warm Soup	d. Teddy Bear

Are You a Mover, Dealer, Holder, or Giver?

Your operating style is your consistent pattern of behavior when interacting with others. There are two inclinations (initiating and sustaining) in this pattern and two tendencies (relational and notional). To determine your tendencies and inclinations, add up the number of a's you marked, then the b's, c's, and d's.

If you marked more a's than anything else, you're a Mover. Movers are highly results-oriented and love to run things their own way. They manage time well and are quite efficient. They are often viewed, however, as unfeeling and threatening in their relationships with others. They have strong initiating tendencies and are oriented to ideas (notional) — in other words, they're more concerned with tangible accomplishments than making people feel good.

If you marked more b's, you're a Dealer. Dealers are quite diplomatic, socially outgoing, and friendly. They get things going, but may settle for less than the best to get on to something else. Dealers tend to manage a situation so they can realize their goals in a socially acceptable way. They have initiating tendencies but are relationally oriented, unlike the more task-oriented movers.

If you marked more c's, you're a Holder. Holders are problem solvers but like to get all the data before making decisions. Some say they're thorough, but others complain that they're slow. Holders value conceptual skills. They may prefer to work alone, and may seem aloof and cool. They value information that allows them to make substantive decisions on the basis of facts and evidence. They are sustainers rather than initiators, and tend to focus on the task rather than people's feelings.

If you marked more d's, you're a Giver. Givers try to minimize conflict and promote everybody's happiness. Many see them as accommodating and friendly, but some see them as wishy-washy. They like to please others and rely on others to give directions about how to get things done. They are sustainers, and their focus is on relations rather than tasks.

What It Means

People with initiating tendencies (Dealers and Movers) are often viewed as more effective in achieving their goals. They're usually the ones who try to get things going and make something happen. Those who have stronger sustaining tendencies (Holders and Givers) are viewed as more effective in supporting others. If you are a Giver or Holder because of your supportive tendencies, you may want to team up with someone who's an initiator, or you may have to expend a bit more energy by initiating a smaller project or two on their own. Notional or task-oriented people might want to try being more friendly and diplomatic with people. Dealers and Givers with strong relational tendencies should strive to be more aware of the procedures, processes, and information that lead to achieving the goal.

Now that you have a better idea about your own personal operating style, you may be able to take more control over how you interact and work with others, and how to get and use information wisely. If you see a need to make some minor adjustments in your style to more effectively "use all your resources and power," now is the time to make those changes.

Finding Levers to be Successful

You're surrounded by resources that will help you achieve your goals. Remember in the Chinese Parable, the young man was admonished to use all of his levers. Below we talk about some of the common levers that exist around you, but which are overlooked by most people.

Don't Overlook Your Neighborhood Levers

Think for a minute about the people with whom you do business almost every week of your life. Do you treat them as friends, as we mentioned earlier? Can they be counted as one of your valuable resources? Consider making a list of these important people who may be able to help you make your life a little more comfortable. We will start the list and you continue it:

Hairdresser/Barber
Service Station Attendant
Pharmacist
Pastor/Spiritual Advisor
Mail Carrier
Travel Agent

Financial Advisor
Supermarket Manager
Doctor
Salesperson (clothing, cars, etc.)
Teachers and principal
Dentist

_____   _____

_____   _____

_____   _____

_____   _____

All of us have special needs and wants. If you travel frequently, make friends with a travel agent. If you have political interests in your community, make friends with those who hold political power. If you like to play racquetball, swim, bike, run, or do marshal arts and fitness programs, become acquainted with various clubs, groups, and people who can encourage you and teach you a particular skill or recreation. Then ask the people you know who might be able to help you reach a particular goal or solve a particular problem.

Levers at Work

Your work place is loaded with resources that can make your life easier and less frustrating. You are surrounded at work by people who have spent years becoming specialists at what they do. Human resource personnel can give you help to accumulate savings, plan for retirement, acquire a loan, obtain medical help for a family member, and even how to survive in a world of job cuts.

Managers can give you insider pointers about what it takes to become a manager in the company. Marketers can help you move from one part of the company to the marketing and sales area, if that is your desire. The key here is to treat everyone as friends and network, network, and network some more. Each company has divisions that do well and others that don't perform as well. Don't wait until the hatchet comes down on your group. Find other places within the company that are prospering and become acquainted with the people in those areas. The easiest thing to do is eat lunch with them and ask questions.

You may even find a number of levers outside of your own company but in a company that has formed an alliance with your company. At one time, several companies were tightly linked together in order to put a new space station in orbit. Considerable cooperation and communication were required between these companies to make the space project a success. This arrangement provides an easy opportunity for workers in one company to talk to workers in one of the other alliance companies. Don't miss out on the levers that are only a lunch or a phone call away.

Professional Groups as Levers

Professional people have organizations that they can join for mutual support. Managers, teachers, hobbyists, trainers, human resource administrators, grocers, meat cutters, truck drivers, refrigerator repair people, law enforcement personnel, physical fitness advocates, and financial planners all have special interest organizations that look after their particular needs. Literally thousands of organizations exist that you can join for networking purposes to get useful information to solve problems and achieve goals.

Most organizations, when you join them, provide a directory that lists members' names and addresses as well as where they are employed. This is a valuable resource because you can call a member working for a company that you might like to work for and ask that person about job opportunities. Also, they may be able to solve a problem that you are having in your company because they've encountered the same problem themselves at an earlier date. This is such an easy way for you to solve problems, but most people never make the call or ask the question!

Most professional groups meet regularly for lunch and to listen to an expert in an area of interest to the organization. This gives you an opportunity to become personally acquainted with other members of the organization and they, then, become a resource that you can draw upon for problem solving, locating work opportunities, or simply connecting socially.

Joining local groups like the PTA, Rotary, Kiwanis, Lions, Exchange, Probus, and Business and Professional Women can provide additional levers.

Two Cautions When Using Levers

Don't become overwhelmed when trying to identify resources. Instead, make a small file of the names of people identified earlier and how to contact them so that you'll be ready when you need assistance in achieving your goals and solving problems. When you have a challenge to overcome or a goal to be achieved, simply thumb through your list for the people who are best qualified to help with your goal. Identify the task that you want to accomplish and where you can use some assistance from others. Remember the success triangle. The more specific the goal, the easier it is to get specific help to reach the goal.

The second caution has to do with asking for help. Here again the suggestion is to be specific. Don't be ambiguous and don't ask for huge requests at the outset. Keep everything simple and specific. When people realize how easy it is to help you, they may be willing to do more at a later time. For example, "I'm building a garage onto my house. Can you give me some help?" If you were a busy contractor or builder, your first response might be, "No way. I'm in my busiest season and this is what I do for a living. I can't go around helping everyone add a garage to their house." To be more specific you might ask yourself what kind of help you could use to build your garage. You may want to ask, "Could you help me purchase materials at a contractor's price? That is a relatively simple request and most contractors and builders can arrange that with one phone call. Do you see the difference in requests? One request is ambiguous and sounds like you are asking for a huge favor, while the second request is simple and quite easy to do.

Most of us like the feeling associated with being supportive and contributing to someone's success. When we make an effort to be helpful, we feel valued and appreciated. Our own challenges become a little lighter because we are serving others. However, most of us feel quite busy and some of us feel more than a little overwhelmed. So put your requests in a form that encourages others to respond in a positive way.

Full Speed Ahead

If you learn how to encourage others to respond positively, you will have learned a great skill for using all your levers: treating others as friends, implementing the success triangle, using your most powerful operating style, and using family, neighborhood, work, and professional resources for assistance. Now move ahead at full speed, using all your levers to improve your life, achieve your goals, and feel calm and collected as you do it. Don't forget to take lots of breaks during the day, reward yourself for completing tasks, and learn how to relax into everything that you do.

In the next chapter we will show you how to become more creative in finding simple and more effective ways to take care of problems and concerns and decrease that overloaded feeling. Unleashing your creative potential is one of the most exciting and profitable things that you will experience in your whole life.

Kick Down the Walls

Time to wake up your creative genius. Why? The answer is simple. There is always a simpler, easier way to do things. You might not have the time to critically analyze a problem and review all the alternative solutions. This is when you need to jump out of the box, knock down the walls that inhibit your thinking and unleash your imagination, intuition, and creative thinking abilities.

This is the third secret of successful and happy people. They don't get hung up on an extensive analysis of a concern or problem. And they don't spend many unhappy and anxious hours brooding over a way to make something better in their lives. They have learned how to loosen up their minds, think more creatively, and swing into action.

This idea is so important, let's repeat it again. There is always a simpler way to do something. There is always an easier way to do something. There is always a more fun way to do something. There is always a more cost effective way to do something. There is always a more efficient way to do something.

Once this idea begins to sink into your brain, your creative potential kicks into action. You approach problems in a more confident and happy way, and you will be surprised at how innovative you can be.

Another important reason to kick down a few walls and wake up your creativity has been expressed by humanistic psychologists. They say "that the ability to dream and imagine must be used and enjoyed for people to experience complete fulfillment in life." Not to create and imagine produces a kind of "creative blackout," which leads to a sense of insecurity and detracts from a person's feelings of confidence, happiness and well being.

If you are already a little discouraged and depressed with parts of your life, unleashing your hidden creative capabilities can bring you a degree of pleasure that is rarely matched by any other experience in life. Acting creatively in even the smallest of matters helps you feel alive and energized. Trying a new hair style or painting a room in a new color does wonders for lifting the spirits of a person who may not have the opportunity to get out of the house very often.

The world is relentless in dumping problems in your lap. The world, however, is not quick at all to provide you with personal solutions. You have to create your own solutions. That's why your engagement in the creative thinking process appears to be the next most necessary and immediate activity for you to consider when trying to become a more successful and happy person. As Albert Einstein once said, "Imagination is more important than knowledge. Knowledge is limited; imagination embraces the world."

Unfortunately, few people really know how they handle problems. They go through life supposing that they are doing one thing, but in actuality they may be doing quite another. Let's take a moment and give you an opportunity to see how you handle daily problems and challenges. All you do is answer five simple questions. Circle the answer that is closest to the way you think you would actually handle the problem.

PERSONAL PROBLEM SOLVING APPROACH QUIZ

1. You had a disagreement with a friend and nothing was resolved.

   a. You return home and try to relax and forget about it.
   b. You talk to another person and discuss possible retaliation.
   c. You work off your frustrations with a brisk walk or other form of exercise.

2. You and your spouse are upset with each other.

   a. You try to calm yourself and not get into any further arguing.
   b. You find a third person so that you can discuss the matter more openly.
   c. You insist on discussing the matter further to find some solution.

3. At your place of employment your leader has created a new policy. You feel it is wrong and will be ineffective.

   a. You hope you're right and pray for the best.
   b. You think that it will change, so you're not going to worry about it.
   c. You go to the leader and try to explain your point of view.

4. You suspect an important promotion is coming up for you.

   a. You consider turning it down because of the increased responsibilities.
   b. You really doubt that you can handle the assignment.
   c. You try to analyze the position and take steps to prepare yourself for it.

5. Your car was damaged in an accident and your insurance doesn't cover the cost of repairs.

   a. You consider dropping the whole insurance policy and having the matter investigated.
   b. You get depressed and complain about it.
   c. You figure out a way to fix the damage.

Once you have completed the questions, look to see which letter (a, b, c,) is the most frequently circled.

If your most frequently circled letter is "a," you tend to run away from problems and fail to acknowledge the real goals in your life that you could or should be achieving. You prefer to head for a closet to get away from trying to accomplish goals or take care of personal concerns.

If "b," then you're the kind of person who complains about problems and attempts to shift responsibility to someone else. Complaining about a situation is far less productive than taking some action to accomplish a goal and resolve a concern.

And, if the letter "c" occurs most in your answers, you're the type of person who likes to take action to identify specific goals and overcome barriers to the achievement of those goals.

Obviously the type "c" approach is the most desirable. It allows you to focus on goals that you want to achieve and to identify the barriers that are keeping you from achieving them. Dealing with challenges, rather than avoiding them, is usually the most desirable way to find happiness and success in life. If you settle for running away from challenges or spending too much energy complaining about them, you become exhausted and unproductive.

The Great Problem Solving Fallacy

Most people think they have a problem when they feel uncomfortable about something. Feeling uncomfortable is NOT a problem. Being upset or uncomfortable is only the effect or manifestation of some barriers to accomplishing a goal. Most people fail to recognize that discomfort comes from the failure to accomplish some goal. You cannot have a problem without having an important goal to achieve. If you think that just feeling upset is a problem, you are engaging in the great problem-solving fallacy.

For example, if, we ask you if you have a problem, you say, "Yes, my problem is my boss." Your response reveals the great problem-solving fallacy, because the boss is actually NOT your problem. Why is that? The reason is that your response fails to indicate what goal you want to achieve. In this context, your goal may be that you want to share some ideas with your boss for improving work conditions, but the boss isn't interested in listening to you. An easy, avoidist way to solve that problem is to stop wanting to share those ideas. However, if you insist on wanting to achieve the goal of sharing a particular type of information with your boss, you still have a problem.

The problem is actually the things that are keeping you from achieving that goal. Why is it that you cannot get your ideas about improving work conditions to your boss? You need to reflect on that issue. It could be that the boss is not interested in changing any work conditions and is actually trying to avoid accomplishing that goal. You and your boss have different goals, so you are probably not going to solve your problem in any direct manner. There may be other things that are not allowing you to achieve your goal, such as the timing of your input to the boss or the manner in which you are trying to present your ideas to your boss. You need to consider as many potential barriers as seem reasonable.

If you decide that the timing of your effort to explain how some work processes can be improved is the primary or major barrier, then you have a specific problem on which to work. Your task is to identify several alternative ways of timing your approach to the boss. One solution to that problem might be to take your boss to lunch and introduce the idea of making some changes in your work at that time.

In solving your problems, the first task is to recognize and state what goals you really want to achieve (see illustration below); the second task is to recognize and state what barriers are keeping you from achieving the goals; and the third task is to make changes in the current situation that help you to overcome the barriers to achieving the goals.

Besides the obvious external rewards that we receive from developing a keener ability to solve problems creatively, there are numerous internal rewards. Being a creative problem-solver is like finding a hidden treasure of happiness and peaceful living. With each creative problem-solving skill that we acquire, we gain a new thrill and enjoyment in daily living. Being creative is fun. Without it, we experience frustration and unrest. Creative people come up with interesting, if not slightly wacky, ideas for accomplishing

| That which you want to achieve | The things that are keeping you from achieving the goal | The steps you take to overcome barriers to achieve the goal |

their goals. Being bored or discouraged does not walk hand in hand with being creative and active. Learning how to be more creative in dealing with your concerns and frustrations is not only important, it is also essential to your success and happiness.

What Is Creativity?

Arthur Koestler, in his classic book *The Act of Creation*, refers to creativity as the actualization of surplus potentials. Other experts call it adeptness in making fresh observations, seeing something in a new way, or as applied imagination. We refer to creativity as kicking down walls and taking a fresh look at everything that comes your way. It is absolutely astounding how energizing it is to try a new way of thinking about something or a new approach to accomplishing something.

If you are a jogger, try changing the route you take. If you drive on the same road to work each day, go down a different street. At work, change your workstation or office around a little. Put something different on the walls if you can. Simple changes are stimulating and invigorating.

After a period of time in which you exercise your mind by handling problems in a more innovative and creative way, you will become more confident and more effective. And, of course, the more effort you devote to understanding how to apply your mind to problems, the greater will be your personal gain.

And let's not forget to say that you don't have to be born smart to be an outstanding creative problem-solver. Research conducted by Sydney Parnes at the Creative Education Foundation at SUNY in Buffalo, NY, and others has demonstrated that almost anyone with the proper training can double his or her ability to produce useful and valuable ideas.

After years of research and experience, psychologists now know that (1) every person can generate hundreds and thousands of worthwhile, useful, personally satisfying ideas, and (2) many methods or approaches can be used to solve problems. That's right, almost any problem can be solved — and usually in a dozen different ways!

Three Creative Approaches

As you discovered in completing Your Personal Problem Solving Approach quiz, when you are faced with a problem or concern, wherever it may occur, don't become emotional and upset about it. Don't try to ignore it and run away from it. And don't waste a lot of time and energy simply complaining about it. Instead, approach each important problem as a challenge, a creative opportunity, and a goal to be achieved. Feel confident that you can solve any problem.

We will now show you three creative problem-solving approaches that you can use in your daily life. What is nice about these approaches is that they can be used quickly and effectively to resolve issues and concerns at work, home, or in the community.

We call the first approach "Back to the Future." It is a simple and easy approach for figuring out how to overcome problems or achieve goals. The second is the "Two-Question Approach" and is a terrific way to stimulate you to think up new ideas and novel ways to solve problems and concerns. And the third technique is called "The Intuition and Inspiration Approach," and it relies on your potential to do visual, creative sensing, and intuitive thinking.

Many artists and scientists use this approach for solving problems and enhancing their creative output.

Back to the Future Approach

To use this approach, locate an "expert" in the area of your problem and interview that person about how he or she solved that problem. Don't just ask anybody. Ask someone who has successfully done what you want to do. Don't be afraid to ask. If you are sincere in needing someone's help, you will be surprised at how much they enjoy sharing their success with you.

Ask that person how the problem was solved or how they achieved the goal. Have a list of potential questions prepared to ask them. Write down their answers in a little notebook that you can refer back to when you're finished. If you have time, ask two or three people how they solved a similar problem or achieved a similar goal.

Later, when you are by yourself, look back over the numerous ideas that you've collected and pick out the single best idea or way or combine a couple of ideas for achieving the goal. The best solution is the one that you can implement with the least amount of effort. When you are generating possible solutions, remember that your best idea may be the third one or the tenth one or the twentieth one. Give yourself a number of ideas to choose from.

The Two-Question Approach

You can be much more creative if you take a moment to separate yourself from the task of achieving a goal and look at what you are doing that might not be fully effective. Psychologists call this "stepping outside of yourself." In management we sometimes call this activity "jumping out of the box." The issue is whether your ideas are flat on the bottom of the box, stuck on the inside of the box, or outside of the box. The "box" represents your current thinking about how to achieve your goals. To get outside the box, you may need to come up with some outlandish ways to achieve your goals.

The axiom in the world of work is that there is always a better way to do something. There is always a simpler way, a more fun way, and a more profitable way to do something. The same axiom applies in your personal life. When you are trying to dig your way out of being overburdened and overloaded, you must approach this goal on the assumption that there is an easier and more effective way to reach your goals.

The way to apply the Two Question Approach is to stop what you are doing for a moment and ask yourself two questions: (1) Why am I doing this? (2) Why am I doing it this way? Let's begin with the first question and consider it from three perspectives by focusing on different parts of the question:

- The first is to focus on the value of what is being done. Is it important? What impact will it have on the goal you are trying to achieve? Make sure you know why it is being done.

- The second looks at who is to do it. Should it really be you, or should it be someone else? Who else could do it? Could someone else do it more effectively? What are the costs of your doing it versus their doing it?

- And the third is to focus on what is being done. Is this the most important thing to do now? Are there other things that are not being done because of this activity?

You will notice that the first form of the question asks why you are doing this, i.e., is this kind of behavior leading to my goal? Sometimes we become involved in an "activity trap." That is, we do things that frequently are low leverage activities and lose out on doing things of greater worth. Be sure to question the value of what you are doing. You may think that what you are doing is important until you realize that no one will care about what you did a hundred years from now.

The second way to ask the question is important at home and at work. In every personal effectiveness seminar we conduct, we encourage parents to look carefully at "why am I doing this." That is, why are you trying to achieve the goal? Invariably, mothers and fathers do things that can be done by their children. Many family scientists claim that children don't know what to do with their spare time and that "children don't learn how to work." Well, here's your chance, Mom and Dad, to look at some of the things you do at home that could be done by your children. Who does the washing and ironing? Hint. Hint. And who takes care of the yard?

This second form of the question is also very important at work. We still have too many managers who do things themselves, because "They want it done right." Our question is, "Are you doing too much yourself?" At work it is extremely important to give others the opportunity to do important tasks and for managers to attend to true leadership activities, like future planning, to make the company more competitive.

The third form of the question simply asks, "Why are you doing this instead of that?" Again, if you are overwhelmed with things to do, why are you doing this thing instead of a more important thing? You can't do it all, so be sure to look at the high priority items and see if they are getting done. You may want to trade a "this" for a higher priority "that."

Let us now consider the second question, "Why am I doing it this way?" Ask yourself the following questions to reveal alternatives for doing the task another way:

- Is there a better way of doing it?
- Is there a faster way of doing it?
- Is there a way of producing better results?
- Is there a more cost-effective way of doing it?
- Is there a more enjoyable way of doing it?
- Is there another creative way of doing it?

Questions like these can stimulate you to think up new ideas and novel ways of doing things. You may even be able to decide whether or not something is worth doing. Asking the two questions is a quick and efficient way to increase creativity at home as well as at work or in the community.

We have been encouraging managers across the world to teach their employees to take "crazy breaks" not passive time-outs but creative time-outs. You should do the same for yourself, your family, and your employees if you are a manager. Realize that there is always a simpler and more fun way to do things that may also save time and money. Teach your family and employees how to use the two-question approach to come up with ideas during a crazy break. They will appreciate the break and thank you for a little more freedom to decide the best way to do things.

The Intuition and Inspiration Approach

Creative ideas and solutions do not always come when you actively concentrate on them. Sometimes they come when you least expect them. Notice these interesting accounts:

When I am, as it were, entirely alone, and of good cheer say, traveling in a carriage, or walking after a good meal, or during the night when I cannot sleep; it is on such occasions that my ideas flow best and most abundantly. Whence and how they come, I know not; nor can I force them. *—Wolfgang Mozart*

While awaiting sleep: Ideas rose in clouds; I felt them collide until pairs interlocked, so to speak, making a stable combination. By the next morning I had established the existence of a class of Fuchsian functions, those which came from the hyper geometric series: I had only to write out the results, which took but a few hours. *—Henri Poincaré (mathematician)*

The words or the language, as they are written or spoken, do not seem to play any role in my mechanism of thought. The psychical entities, which seem to serve as elements in thought, are certain signs and more or less clear images which can be voluntarily reproduced and combined. *—Albert Einstein*

The painter passes through states of fullness and emptying. That is the whole secret of art. I take a walk in the forest of Fontainebleau. There I get an ingestion of greenness; I must empty this sensation into a picture. The painter paints as if in urgent need to discharge himself of his sensations and his vision! *—Picasso*

I shut my eyes for a few minutes, with my portable typewriter on my knee. I make my mind a blank and wait and then, as clearly as I would see real children, my characters stand before me in my mind's eye. The story is enacted almost as if I had a private cinema screen there ... I am in the happy position of being able to write a story and read it for the first time at one and the same moment. *—Enid Blyton (author)*

Albert Einstein once said, "I believe in intuition and inspiration; at times I feel certain I am right while not knowing the reason." Since the "inspired moment" of the musician, artist, and scientist most often occurs at such odd times, we generally refer to it as a nondeliberate act. It seems like we have such little control over the "ah ha" experience that we relegate it to the area of luck or happy accident. Indeed, what happens is usually beyond our conscious control and frequently happens when we think that we are not attending to a problem at all.

Housewives, students, businessmen, writers, Nobel prize recipients, and children alike report the inspiration or sudden insight they receive when walking, sleeping, relaxing, or in some other unusual state of consciousness. What is truly exciting is that much research, including our own research in biofeedback, demonstrates that almost anyone can learn how to produce such a creative state.

Put "Ah Ha!" to Work for You

Ponder your unachieved goal. Study it from a variety of angles. Inspirational insight doesn't usually come to people who haven't thought deeply about what they are attempting to achieve.

Now stop thinking about it. Forget about it for a few days and let your subconscious do its work. Sometimes great thoughts come to you when you are sleeping or in the morning when you are waking. Or you can accelerate the process by relaxing, freeing your mind from worry and anxiety, and disconnecting from the world a little bit, or meditating.

To encourage this kind of creative inspirational activity, follow these steps:

1. Find a quiet place where you will not be interrupted for a few minutes.

2. Close your eyes, relax your facial muscles, breathe slowly, and place a specific unachieved goal or concern lightly upon your mind. Don't think about it; just let it be there ready to connect with any impression or image that presents itself in your relaxed state. Allowing an idea to form takes different amounts of time. But when it happens, you will know it. You may find a great feeling of elation or you may simply say, "That's so simple, I can't believe that I didn't think of it before."

3. Write it down! Ideas are such fragile things that they often leave your mind as quickly as they enter. Don't get caught thinking that you had a great idea last night, but you can't remember what it was. Write it down. Einstein wrote down his thoughts. Edison sketched out his ideas. Da Vinci's notebooks are world famous.

Francis Bacon, a 17th century English official who helped usher in the modern age of science, once said that "a man would do well to carry a pencil in his pocket, and write down the thoughts of the moment. Those that come unsought for are commonly the most valuable, and should be secured, because they seldom return."

Implement Your Ideas

This is the last step in creative problem solving. This is the action step that makes it all worth the effort. Many people come to this point in solving problems and stop. They have good ideas, but they do precious little about implementing them.

We will never forget the millionaire whom we invited to speak to one of our university business classes. Near the end of his presentation, the millionaire looked at the rather large class of students and said, "Everyone in this room has a million-dollar idea. Statistically speaking, however, no one in this room will become a millionaire. Do you know why? Because none of you will take the time to implement your million-dollar idea."

This goal-achieving step should be approached just as vigorously and creatively as other parts of the creative thinking process. You must figure out all the ways you can for putting your ideas into practice, overcoming objections to them, and ensuring that they will be effective. Ideas can be implemented in many ways:

- Determine how a similar idea was implemented successfully in the past.

- Ask a successful person how she/he did it.

- Read some specific information about how to do it.

- Stimulate your mind by asking yourself questions like these: Who might help? What resources are available? When and where should I start?

- Do some "reverse brainstorming" by trying to figure out what might go wrong. You should address those preliminary concerns before pursuing your goal directly.

- Decide, finally, what the easiest, simplest, first step should be in implementing your idea.

- Take action.

Alex F. Osborn, who has been called the "father of brainstorming," once said "a fair idea put to use is better than a good idea kept on the polishing wheel." Consider the idea that nothing much happens if you don't implement your creative ideas. In fact, if you master the approaches we have just described, you should be able to achieve many practical goals that you were unable to achieve earlier.

Much of the fun of getting up in the morning is to see what ideas come to mind during the day that can be used to reduce some of the frustrations associated with life. If you put yourself in a creative state of mind, you will be surprised at how many good ideas can come to you. When those ideas present themselves to you, be sure to write them down so that you won't forget them.

To get rid of the boredom, repetition, and some of the frustration that is present in your life, be creative by taking a fresh look at everything that comes your way. Life will never be boring again, nor will it be overwhelming.

Close Your Company Store

Have you ever eaten shaved ice at Matsumoto's on the north shore of Oahu, Hawaii? It's the best shaved ice in the world.

Matsumoto's is a rustic, small store located in Haleiwa right alongside Highway 83. People come from all over the world go there. To reach the back of the store, you have to wend your way around various counters and obstacles. If you like, and we highly recommend it, you can have a scoop of vanilla ice cream put into the bottom of a cup. Then the shaved ice is placed on top of the ice cream. And finally several knock-your-eyes-out sweet syrups are squeezed onto the shaved ice. A little spoon and straw are pushed into the treat of your life. Since there is no place in the store to eat, you have to go out the back door and stand in the dirt or go back out the front door and sit on an old wooden bench.

Several years ago we had been attending meetings in Waikiki and were driving back to our sleeping quarters in La'ie. It was late in the afternoon, quite warm, and we were anxious to make a stop at Matsumoto's before returning to our evening's lodging. We drove up to the store and parked just across the street. We walked across the street to get a shaved ice treat and Mr. Matsumoto came out on the little wooden porch, picked up the bench that sat in front of the store, waved at us, and went inside and locked the door. It was 5 p.m.

We were dumbfounded. It didn't seem to matter that he was turning away customers. It also didn't seem to matter that he was sending a lot of business down the street to his competitors. We mumbled something to each other, vowed to come back earlier next time, and drove off.

Twice is Enough

About a half of a block from our college campus was a small store called the Bamboo Hut. The food was a kind of Hawaiian-Chinese conglomeration consisting of rice, noodles, chicken (legs, wings, and large pieces), pork, wontons, vegetables, pork, gravy and a variety of drinks. Delicious food and tons of it heaped on your plate for a very low price. The store was little and old, with a number of small tables set up inside on which to eat.

Students, faculty, cheerleaders, football players and towns-people flocked to the store during the lunch period. In fact, there always seemed to be a line of people backed up from the serving counter, down the aisle, and out onto the sidewalk. Much of the time, more people were lined up outside of the hut than were inside. We were amazed that so many people came to eat at this rather small food establishment.

Again, we were treated to the "Matsumoto experience." Only this time, at two o'clock the "closed sign" was put in the window and shortly thereafter the doors were locked. This surprised those of us who are filled with that capitalistic spirit. Why would anyone doing that much business open the store at 11 a.m. and close the store three hours later at 2 p.m.? And, by the way, the Bamboo Hut didn't open on Saturdays or Sundays at all.

Our first thought was that we needed to talk to the owner and see if we could franchise this concept. Any store that can do that kind of business in such a short period of time would probably be a gold mine if the hours and days were extended.

The owner was a quiet, well-mannered person of Hawaiian descent who answered to the name of "Tom Tom." One day we introduced ourselves and asked him why he shut down his store so early when it was obvious that he could serve many more customers and probably make a larger profit by staying open longer. "It is enough," he said.

"What does *it* mean?" he was asked.

With an amused look on his face, Tom Tom said that he made enough money in three hours to pay the bills and have enough extra to take care of his family and enjoy other things in life.

Set a Stop Time

Now you understand the title of this chapter. Most people have not learned to close their "company store." They haven't decided when enough is enough. All of us need to set a stop time, a time when we quit working, stop doing things for others, and set aside time for ourselves. If we don't, we will go each day until we drop exhausted into the bed and eventually find ourselves in a real emotional and physical mess.

Let's face it, our minds and bodies can't take a continual pounding. Eventually we'll have a breakdown. Don't wait for a midlife crisis or sickness to force you to close your company store.

Do it while you still have your health and can make a voluntary decision. Remember, you can't do it all. You have to let go of something. Learn to close your company store now before you are forced to because of the onset of depression or some other malady.

Put a Sign on Yourself

Several years ago people attending a workshop questioned whether they could "close their company store." They said their children needed their help well into the late evening. Some of the fathers were having a hard time keeping up with the demands of work and were bringing home reports that they could fill out and take back to work in the morning. It didn't seem as though anyone knew how to simply and decisively close their company store.

Suddenly, a mild-mannered, middle-aged lady stood up and said, "It's easy to close your company store. I started to do it a few years ago. It's simple, and it's a lifesaver for me." Of course, everyone quieted down and focused their attention on the lady.

She explained that she was a mother of several children and had a hard-working husband. She said that she was staying up all hours of the night trying to do things for her children and husband, and generally trying to help others who needed her help. She realized that if she kept up her nighttime efforts, she would soon be fatigued and discouraged during the day and probably turn into a tired old witch. She also mentioned that she didn't have much of an opportunity to read anything of her own interest, work on any personal projects, or just take time to relax and think quietly by herself.

Everyone wondered how she had gotten out of this personal

time trap. No one realized that she had previously attended a seminar like the one being presented. She explained that she took a piece of poster paper 8 inches by 3 inches and wrote on it: "Company Store Closed." Then she tied a piece of yarn on each end so that she could put it over her head and hung it on her chest. She explained to her husband and children that she needed some time for herself each day.

She explained to them that she would help until 9 p.m., after which she would put on her sign. The audience laughed. She said it only took a few days before everyone realize that she was serious. Soon, the children, as well as her husband, made sure that they approached her for help before 9 p.m. She concluded her comments by saying that this was probably the single best thing she ever did in her life in terms of digging out from under all the demands that were placed on her.

When you decide to close your company store, you learn that you have more anxiety about it than other family members. In the beginning, you may discover that you want to get up and do something to help someone, or you remember some household tasks that need to be done and you want to attend to them. In other words, you may be your own worst enemy and feel a little anxiety about instituting this change in your life. If you need to, say to yourself or put up a note that says, "I have had a good day and helped and encouraged others. Now it's my time to enjoy the rest of the evening." Don't give up. Set a time to stop and stick to it. Before long, the family will run smoothly and you will look forward to having time to do your own things or even do nothing, if that is what you desire.

Prioritize and Delegate

At work, you may frequently find yourself in the same situation as at home, working your head off when someone else should be completing the assignment, researching a project, and growing in the process. Look around, especially if you are in a supervisory or management position. What are you doing that someone else could be doing? Ask yourself the golden question: Why am I doing this?

Our research shows that people in leadership positions need to quit doing things that others can do and start doing things that others cannot do. Are you so busy that you don't have time to listen to workers' suggestions or time for long range planning? If you are, you need to redirect others and involve them more effectively in getting work goals accomplished.

The worst way to redirect is to command someone to do something. In the Japanese work world, a manager or leader who has to command people to do things is considered a failure. You are a failure because you have not taken the time to develop a trusting relationship with your workers. And you may not have taken the time to demonstrate that what you are asking them to do fits nicely into the company goals and will bring good rewards to the work group.

No one likes to be constantly commanded to do things. Most people like to be asked to do things. "Could you," "Can you," and "Would you" are simple ways to avoid coming down rather hard on people with a command. Asking shows respect for other people and even gives them an opportunity to improve upon the way a task could be done.

If you are a pushing and controlling manager or parent, your employees or children will start to push back and resent being told what to do. Employees catch on rather quickly to your "asking" approach, and they appreciate being treated as grown-ups. Children may not realize that such expressions as "could you" and "would you" actually mean to do the task right away. However, once they understand the softer, kinder approach that you are using, most children will feel the difference between being asked to do something and being strongly commanded to do something.

Close Your Store Several Times During The Day

Find at least an occasion or two when you can enjoy some quiet time every day. Closing your company store before the moon gets high in the sky is great and is, of course, a first priority for you. However, that is not enough to maintain a semblance of sanity in your life. You must also learn to find a few minutes of time each day and preferably two or three times a day, to take a mini break and relax. Just shut your office or bedroom door or sit in your car for a few minutes before going into a store or into your house. Close your eyes, breathe slowly from your diaphragm, and let the cares of the world fade away. Sounds simple doesn't it? But guess what?

Most People Don't Know How To Relax!

In some of our research on anxiety, hundreds of subjects have been connected to biofeedback machines. In each experiment, we connected various individuals to an electromyograph to measure tension in the frontalis muscles, which are controlled by the voluntary nervous system. We can consciously control our muscles. The frontalis muscle tension level is a pretty good indication of stress in the upper part of your body.

In the same experiment, we connected each subject to an external digital thermometer. With the subject's hand connected through a transducer to a temperature biofeedback machine, we were able to measure anxiety as it is represented in the autonomic nervous system, which is the system of nerves that control involuntary functions.

We wired each subject to a machine and gave them a few minutes to relax. We asked them to tell us when they felt relaxed. When they told us they were relaxed, we took a reading from the frontalis muscle and from the digital temperature machine. Guess what? When the subjects said that they were relaxed, the sensitive measuring instruments showed quite a contrary result. Most of the subjects weren't anywhere near relaxed. However, with a little instruction, practice, and persistence, each subject was able to attain a useful level of relaxation.

Time Out!

Before we go any further, let's take a time out right now and learn how to relax. For a minute or two, we would like you to stop feeling responsible for everyone and everything around you. See if you can just enjoy this very moment. Find a place where you can sit comfortably without any distractions. Turn off the radio, television, computer, and phone.

Sit so that your feet are on the floor. If you can, take off your shoes and socks, and loosen your belt or skirt a little. And if your shirt or blouse is pressing tightly against your neck, you should undo the top button. Sit with your back against the back of the chair, with your upper body now resting comfortably and balanced on your hips so that if you were to fall asleep you would not fall off the chair.

Allow your eyes to close. Don't force your eyes to close. Allow them to slowly close as you relax your eyes. With your eyes relaxed and lids closed, relax your face. Make a grimace and then let your facial muscles relax. Feel the tension leave your face. Tighten the muscles in your arms and then relax them. Do the same for your hips. Tighten your buttocks so as to rise up a little. Now relax those muscles and feel the tension leave. Remember, as you go through this process of learning how to relax, don't tighten up a muscle group that you have just relaxed. This is where a little practice and training come in. Relax each of the muscle groups once and do not tense them up again as you go to another group.

Now, tense up your calf muscles and relax them. Do the same thing with your toes: curl them up and then unfold and relax them. Feel relaxation from the crown of your head to the soles of your feet. If a muscle group is a bit stubborn, return quickly to that group, tighten up, and then relax that muscle group.

This next step is quite important in learning how to relax. Take a comfortably deep breath, hold it for three seconds, and exhale. If you can, try to breathe through your nose.

Try also to breathe in and out like a baby. This is called "belly breathing." This is what you do when you lay on your back. Try to avoid lifting your shoulders when you breathe. This is called "chest breathing" or up and down breathing and is not very relaxing.

Each time you exhale, feel your anxieties, worries, and concerns leave you. Do this a few times and repeat those lines quietly to yourself:

"I feel comfortable and warm."

"I feel relaxed and quiet."

"I feel very peaceful and comfortable."

The more you follow these instructions for mini-time-outs, the more quickly you enter a calm, relaxed state of mind, and the more you enjoy a moment of complete serenity. Soon, with a little practice, you can feel your mind relax and become peaceful.

Take a short relaxation break right now. Don't be afraid to shut out the world for a minute or two. Reread the instructions and try it. Feel the relief you receive from your short break. Savor this very moment. When you've taken a quiet, warm and comfortable relaxation break, come back and read a little more.

Now that you've learned how to close your company store and take an effective mini time out, we would like you to understand this next important sanity-saving idea.

Learn to Relax Into Everything You Do

In a seminar in Mission Bay, Calif., Theodore Barber, a renowned experimental hypnotist, was discussing the topic of hypnosis and psychosomatics. He suggested to us that people often do things in such a quick way that they can't remember, much less enjoy, what they did.

He asked his audience if they could even remember the refreshing feeling derived from their last drink of water from a drinking fountain. Audience members had done it so unconsciously and quickly that they couldn't remember when they last took a drink of water, much less how it felt. He suggested that children experience a similar lack of memory when they eat supper. They rush through the meal so quickly, they forget to taste the food. A short time after the meal is finished, the kids are back looking in the refrigerator for something to eat. They can hardly remember what a delicious meal they just had. Sometimes they can't even remember that they just ate about 20 minutes ago.

He suggested that we slow down and relax even when we are taking a drink from a water dispenser. He urged us to feel the coolness of the water and enjoy the water moving down our throats to our stomach. He said that we could turn a drink of water into our favorite meal.

In the similar vein, judge Oliver Wendell Holmes suggested that people should "take a music bath once or twice a week for a few seasons; you will find that it is to the soul what the water-bath is to the body."

Allow More Time for the Task

Have you noticed how many people rush from one task to the next? They push their way through a task as fast as they can so that they can get on to the next one. You don't do that, do you? If you do, you are missing one of the simplest ways to relax into everything you do.

It takes about five minutes to walk from our offices at the university to the locker room in the physical education building. Many faculty and staff work out during their lunch period. Some like to jog, others play basketball and racquetball, and still others like to lift weights and do marshal arts. The most amazing thing happens when class ends at 11:50 a.m. and the lunch period starts. The faculty and staff almost on a mutually understood signal, rush out of their rooms and offices and head to the locker rooms.

They quickly change into their workout clothes, exercise, and then shower and quickly return to work. All in an hour. Frenetic is an understatement.

Contrast that with the person — and there are a few — who allows fifteen minutes, not five, to get to the locker room. This person is walking, not running. This person is feeling the sun on her neck, enjoying the sunshine, smelling the flowers, and talking to students and friends on the way. Upon arriving at her locker, she enjoys taking off her more formal teaching attire, getting rid of the scarf and blouse and putting on her workout clothes. This person relaxes into her workout, as we have said, stays comfortable and happy, doesn't compete ferociously, but does her best, and seems to get along with everyone.

After the workout, she returns to her locker, takes off her sweats, and takes a warm and long shower. She seems to enjoy putting on her working clothes and, somewhat casually, walking off to find and enjoy a little food and then go back to her office. These more relaxed people present quite a contrast to those who are rushing through their lunch and exercise ritual.

Allowing more time than what the circumstance might require becomes especially important when getting up in the morning and preparing to go to work. We are always amazed at the tension and anxiety that is created when people don't get up early enough to groom themselves properly. They don't eat a good breakfast, listen to some good music, take care of any important household matters, say good bye to the children and spouse, and leave early enough so that delays in traffic won't make them late for work.

A young daughter of a good friend of ours said that her dad always took the time to see her for a moment before he left for work. She said that her dad told her two things: "Remember who you are" and "Make it a great day!" She said, "Being reminded of those two things each morning by a father who loved me, and would take the time to kiss me goodbye, has made all the difference in my life."

If you are one of those people who don't allow enough time to get up, enjoy the morning, and get to work on time, then make a change now. For most people, getting up just twenty minutes earlier and relaxing into going to work can make a significant difference in getting rid of those overwhelmed feelings. Your spouse and children will quickly notice the difference and you will feel the difference.

You may be thinking, "The problem is that I don't have enough time to allow more time for various tasks." Most of us have experienced that same kind of thinking. That's why we've been making suggestions in this book about how you can't do it all, although you can do the important things. You can be more creative, use the many resources available to make your life easier and pretty much take care of most of what is worth doing.

In this chapter, we've suggested that you close your company store, prioritize a little, delegate more effectively, take some time-outs, and relax into everything you do. All these suggestions work together in a holistic manner. Each suggestion makes it possible to achieve the next one. You have enough time for what is important to you. As we illustrated in the first chapter, all of us have a chance to make choices about how we use our time because it is our choice.

Grab Your Oxygen First

Every time you get on an airplane you hear the flight attendant advise you that, should an emergency situation arise, you should put on your own oxygen mask before you take care of others. That's good advice, not only on an airplane but in everyday living, too. If you don't "put on your own oxygen mask first," you run a much greater risk of fatigue, burn out, and discouragement.

What Is Your No. 1 Priority?

During our last dozen management seminars, we took the time to ask, "What is a manager's No. 1 priority?" It is important to point out that we are not talking about a manager's major responsibility. Instead, we're referring to his or her No. 1 priority." Although we received hundreds of sincere responses dealing with various aspects of management and leadership, none of the seminar participants were anxious to suggest that they themselves should be their first priority.

After some discussion, however, most participants realized that if they didn't figure out a way to regenerate themselves daily, they would succumb to the great demands and responsibilities placed upon them. You are no different. If you don't keep yourself strong in body and mind, you may become more vulnerable to emotional duress, fatigue, and disease. When you become tired and overwhelmed with obligations, you become tense and terse in your comments and less patient with others. Your ability to govern your thoughts and maintain control over your life is weakened.

To live life effectively, especially during periods of disappointment and overload, you must master the basic principles of physical regeneration and self-renewal. You must not ignore opportunities to relax with family and friends, eat nourishing food, and sleep after a day of work. Observing the laws of health — which includes good eating habits, sleep, and exercise — and developing positive thinking patterns are absolutely fundamental to keeping yourself healthy.

In addition, you should continue to develop an inner strength that comes from a clear standard of morality of mind and action. If you live life in conflict with your core values, you will experience distress, ill health, and, often, deep regret. You have enough challenges from outside of yourself that you don't need additional stress coming from your own inner conflicts. Like the song says, "We're not trying to make angels out of you, since angels are so few, so until an authentic angel comes along, we'll string along with you."

Strengthen Your Physical Self

Let's consider your outward or physical strength first. To physically strengthen yourself and enhance your ability to cope with a sometimes unfriendly environment, focus on these four fundamental ideas:

You are what you eat.
You are how you exercise.
You are how you sleep.
You are what you think.

Each of these four factors is important to your health and well being. What you do in one of these four areas supports and enhances the other three areas. Together, they form a synergistic relationship and a more holistic approach to strengthening yourself. In that holistic approach, the sum, of course, becomes greater than the parts. You might think that you are stronger with four parts than you are with only one, two, or three, but with four parts you are five times stronger.

Physical Wellness Test

You probably don't have a systematic way of assessing how well you're doing in terms of your health practices. This quiz is designed to give you a quick profile of where you stand in relation to the four critical factors for maintaining your physical and mental strength. By answering the following questions truthfully, you will be able to pin point areas where you may want to make some improvements as well as identify areas where you're doing well.

Don't ponder the items. Sit back, relax, grab a pencil, and quickly check off your responses. To complete the quiz, circle the answers that most accurately describe the way you're presently attending to your health needs. When you've completed the quiz, analyze the scores according to the instructions below.

THE HEALTH QUIZ

F = Frequently	0 = Occasionally		N = Not Usually		
1. I express optimistic statements to my friends.			F	O	N
2. I relax with friends and family members.			F	O	N
3. I eat nourishing food.			F	O	N
4. I take a brisk walk or engage in other physical activities daily.			F	O	N
5. I avoid caffeine and sugar in drinks like coffee and cola.			F	O	N
6. I avoid medications like tranquilizers and sleeping pills.			F	O	N
7. I sleep through the night.			F	O	N
8. I avoid smoking.			F	O	N
9. I use a form of deep relaxation to truly relax.			F	O	N
10. I avoid drinking alcohol.			F	O	N
11. I eat fresh fruits, vegetables, and salads.			F	O	N
12. I avoid eating "fast foods" and "junk food."			F	O	N
13. I feel and act optimistically.			F	O	N

Scoring instructions: Give each circled "F" a score of 3 points; each "O" 2 points; and each "N" 1 point. Now total the scores.

- An "A" score would be in the 34 to 39 range.
- A "B" score would be in the 28 to 33 range.
- A "C" score would be in the 22 to 27 range.
- A "D" score would be in the 16 to 21 range.
- A "F" score would be below 16.

How close did you come to an "A" score?
You may have a little fixing up to do with regards to

maintaining your health and physical strength. To strengthen yourself on a daily basis, consider the suggestions that we make in the following sections.

You Are What You Eat

In 1825, Jean Anthelme Brillat-Savarin, the famous French epicure and gastronome, reportedly said: "Tell me what you eat, and I will tell you what you are." Although the essence of people cannot be reduced simply to what they eat, food can have a significant impact on behavior.

For example, contrary to popular opinion, foods that are high in sugar can significantly reduce your energy level. Think about the amount of candy, soda pop, ice cream, cupcakes, doughnuts, cake, pie, and other sweets you eat. If you have time, make a list of all the sweets you eat in a day. Eating sweets raises blood-sugar levels, and the body tries to get rid of the excessive sugar. Your pancreas will release a large amount of insulin to get the sugar out of the blood. When you eat sweets, you may experience a little burst of energy, but it will usually be followed by a dull and tired feeling and possibly a headache. You don't have to abstain from all sweets, but you should taper off and replace as many as you can with less sugary foods, like fresh fruit or a slice of raisin bread.

Most books on the subject of proper eating habits also say that people have more energy if they reduce or eliminate fatty foods, such as whole dairy products (milk and cheese), fatty cuts of meat, fried foods, hamburgers and shakes. Complex carbohydrates found in vegetables, beans, grains, pasta, cereals, breads, potatoes, rice and fruits boost your energy as well as help you keep your weight under control. Of course, even the good foods should be eaten in moderation.

Don't skip meals. Your body needs an adequate supply of energy. Running off to work with nothing but a cup of coffee in your system is absolutely inappropriate for good energy levels. And while we are on the subject, if you are drinking a lot of cola drinks, coffee, tea, and other fluids that have caffeine in them, start tapering off as soon as possible. Caffeine drinks are stimulants and frequently force us into a psychological dependency, only to deliver a brief energy boost. Better to snack on a bagel or low fat yogurt.

A good diet starts the day with a light, healthy breakfast. Think of oatmeal, Cream-of-Wheat, whole-grain cereal, a bagel, skim or low-fat milk, fruit, fruit juice, low fat yogurt, or waffles and pancakes.

For lunch, consider such items as chili, sourdough bread, sliced turkey breast on a sandwich with lettuce, tomato and low-fat mayonnaise, vegetables, soup, and hot rolls. Eat lightly in the middle of the day to avoid that tired sluggish feeling in the afternoon. Take relaxation breaks to help you focus on eating right. When you make effective changes, reward yourself with a visit to the hairdresser, or a new dress, or go to a movie, or work on a hobby. It is, of course, not a good idea to reward yourself with a big blast of sugar, fat, and calories.

Live it up at suppertime with good, energizing foods and you will be surprised at how alive you feel during the rest of the evening. Try such foods as baked or broiled fish, steamed or stir-fried vegetables, baked potatoes with low fat sour cream, pasta topped with tomato sauce and a tossed salad, a delicious casserole with whole wheat bread, or great lasagna with an Italian salad. Just open any housekeeping magazine for a whole array of delicious, healthy meals that are perfect for suppertime. Remember, you don't need to eat a lot of food to be healthy. So, eat moderately, eat slowly, and enjoy the delicious tastes!

Glenn Ford, a famous movie star and a man who worked at a pace that most stars half his age would find exhausting, was asked about his energy secrets. He said: "I swim in my pool every day, and I eat lots of proteins and a lot of fish. But I never eat white bread, chocolate, desserts, sweets, sugar, or any kind of junk food." Maybe a simple "Glenn Ford" diet overhaul would help your physical health.

If you are a smoker, a heavy drinker, or a drug user, please give up these bad habits. They are all detrimental to your health. Find a program, a mentor, and a specific plan for stopping. Use recreational activities and relaxation programs to relieve the tensions. If you are an addict, please be sure to find a competent professional who can supervise your withdrawal efforts. As Confucius once said, "A man who has committed a mistake and doesn't correct it is committing another mistake."

You Are How You Exercise

Everyone should exercise. Walking, playing tag, gardening, biking, or playing golf for at least one hour a day helps keep off excess pounds. These are some of the conclusions reached recently by the National Academy of Science's Institute of Medicine. In 1996 the Surgeon General's report recommended a minimum of 30 minutes of moderate exercise. The new report says that 30 minutes is good, but an hour is better for controlling weight gain and lowering the risk of cardiovascular disease.

Activities can include mopping floors, jumping rope, or playing tennis, and the 60 minutes can be accumulated in 10- to 15-minute increments. The whole idea is that you need to be more active. You may not meet the 30 minutes of recommended activity in your present way of life, and you will definitely not meet the 60 minutes recommended unless you find something that you really enjoy doing and are willing to stick to it for awhile.

Research has demonstrated that exercise and physical activity can ease tension and reduce the amount of stress that you feel. The beautiful part about exercise is that it takes only 30 minutes a day to be effective, but it must be regular.

In our own literature research, we discovered that the first three benefits of exercise have little to do with improving the cardiovascular system. Instead, exercise has other benefits, including (1) a healthier self-concept — you feel better about yourself; (2) a reduction in overall stress and anxiety — you feel less depressed and worried; and (3) increased self-confidence — you feel more self-assured and positive.

Brisk walking, jogging, cycling, dancing, swimming, and competitive sports are all useful ways of strengthening your body. The real secret is to choose activities that you enjoy doing. Then learn to relax into them and do them regularly. If you need encouragement, go with people who enjoy a similar activity. Set small goals at first. Try not to miss an exercise session. When you feel progress, reward yourself with time to relax and enjoy your success. Don't compete with anyone. Just enjoy yourself. This commitment is for your own health's sake.

No matter what you do, start slowly. Take jogging or fast walking for example. Millions of people enjoy jogging. It is something you can do almost anyplace at anytime that is convenient for you. It only takes a good pair of shoes. No other special equipment is required. You can start jogging by yourself at your own pace and for your own distance. You don't need anyone else around unless you think that you'd be more consistent if you jogged with someone. Keeping track of how long you jog or how far you go is also very easy.

Start slowly. You're not competing with anyone. Stay within the "bounds of your breath." Stop when you feel uncomfortable. Then, try it again later in the day or tomorrow. Whether or not you want to improve your ability to walk fast or jog, you will improve only if you persist. Pretty soon you'll see yourself moving along at a rate that amazes you and results in a heart rate of around 100 to 140 beats per minute.

If you take the slow and easy but regular approach to exercise, you will turn agony into a pleasurable experience. Soon you'll notice that you are going a little farther or a little faster. You will notice, before long, that you have more energy and don't feel like stopping so soon. You may even want to engage in other physical activities because of all the benefits that you're feeling.

Many walkers, joggers, and exercisers experience not only more energy and alertness, but also report feeling happier and more cheerful. Others report better coordination, and some even see improvements in their body shape. Some smokers, who are trying to quit smoking, report that their body feels cleaner after running and they have less desire to dirty it up again with tobacco smoke. Still others report that the exhilaration of exercising seems to decrease their need for drinking alcohol products. Putting regular exercise in your daily routine is a great way to live life to its fullest.

You Are How You Sleep

Rest and sleep rejuvenate you. Even if you are not an athlete, you know the connection between good sleep and good performance. You probably know that sleep is basic to everything you do, whether it's at the office, home, or on the tennis court. Early to bed and early to rise, but don't sleep longer than necessary, is still the best advice. Some feel that late to bed and late to rise also meets the basic requirements, if you have the life style to support such a pattern, but late to bed and early to rise is simply not effective.

The National Sleep Foundation reports, however, that one in three people suffer bouts of sleeplessness. And almost everyone experiences a little trouble snoozing occasionally. If you are one of those people who go to bed, turn off the lights, slide under the covers, and find yourself staring into the darkness, unable to go to sleep, there are a few things that you can do to remedy the problem. One solution is to stay up until you get sleepy. You may be a night person.

Are stressors keeping you awake? The most common reason you don't sleep well is because you are worried about something. If you find yourself unable to sleep, take a good look at your life. Are you worried about a relationship with a friend or your spouse? Are you worried about a child or your job? Are you bothered because you have too much to do? Is your financial situation bothering you? Any one of these stressful situations can cause you to lose precious sleep.

If problems and concerns begin to crowd into your mind, don't panic. Think about these concerns for a few minutes. Decide what you might do about them tomorrow. That's right. Tell yourself that you can't do much about anything tonight. But you will attend to those nagging thoughts tomorrow.

Then put a smile back on your face and possibly a little song in your heart. Relax and allow yourself to drift off to a peaceful sleep. There is little doubt that if stress is the cause of sleep loss, decreasing the intensity of the stressors will significantly increase the quality of your rest.

Is caffeine the problem? Gradually cutting down on your intake of caffeine should allow you to sleep more deeply. Caffeine is the stimulant contained in colas, chocolate, tea, and coffee. Stop drinking caffeine products at 2 p.m. in the afternoon. If you're a coffee drinker, limit yourself to no more than a couple of cups per day. Remember, many medications, diet aids, decongestants, and pain relievers contain caffeine and may keep you up at night. Take pills at least four hours before you try to sleep.

Are you short on third-stage deep sleep? If you seem to be sleeping for an adequate amount of time, but still feel quite tired after arising in the morning, you may be short on third-stage deep sleep. Doctors of internal medicine explain that (a) if you feel cold during the night, or are awakened by sounds, or by an uncomfortable pillow or mattress, or (b) if deep anxieties keep returning you to levels of light sleep or awaken you, then you need to make some immediate changes to increase deep sleep. If you need help getting the rest that comes from increased deep sleep, you may obtain help from your physician or even a short visit to a psychiatrist. There are even some new medical helps that can be useful in regulating sleep.

Are you getting your body ready for sleep? Doing regular exercise during the day is a great help in preparing your body to enter a restful sleep, but finish your exercising at least three hours before you intend to go to sleep. That is, exercise at five-thirty in the evening for half an hour and go to bed at nine. Don't eat a big meal or spicy foods at night. Your stomach will work overtime trying to digest everything while you are trying to get to sleep.

Your stomach will start to burn and you will usually lose the battle. You will pay the price of late evening eating.

The Better Sleep Council experts say that another way to get your body ready for sleep is to establish a regular time to go to bed and get up in the morning — including weekends. The weekend sleep-in syndrome won't allow you to catch you up on the sleep you miss during the week. Erratic sleeping habits can be a real energy-drain. If you need to, establish a little bedtime ritual like taking a warm bath, reading a short story, or spending a few moments remembering all the wonderful things in life that you are grateful for. Don't try to force yourself to sleep. The more you try, the harder it will become.

Some people set an alarm clock before they go to sleep, but then stay awake worrying about whether it will go off on time. Stop worrying, just set the alarm on your clock, then hide the clock in a drawer, and relax.

Healthy people only need about eight hours of sleep. Many people over fifty seem to do nicely on about six to seven hours of sleep. Experiment a little bit and see what you actually need. Don't worry about how much sleep other people need. Develop your own ritual for going to sleep.

What's the story on "power naps"? A power nap consists of taking a short, but totally quiet snooze. This is a somewhat controversial topic. Do they work or don't they? How long should a power nap be? If you are not sleeping comfortably at night, you probably ought to skip the afternoon siesta, and see if you can go to bed "tired." However, if you are sleeping comfortably at night, but you do not feel quite as alert and tend to perform at a lower level than you would like during the day, you may want to experiment a little with a power nap.

Much of the controversy concerning power naps is over the amount of time that one should sleep during the day. Some sleep experts believe that anything less than a good 45-minute snooze is not useful because, as we mentioned earlier, the body doesn't have enough time to go into deep sleep.

Others believe that 20 minutes might be helpful, but that power naps over 2 hours in length should be avoided, since when you wake up, you'll feel more confused than refreshed. Since there are so many differences in each individual's physiological state, the best advice is to experiment a little and try to discover what works best for you. Consider the tranquil appeal of this poetic verse by Robert Louis Stevenson:

The day returns and brings us the petty round of irritating concerns and duties. Help us to play the man [woman], help us to perform them with laughter and kind faces; let cheerfulness abound with industry. Give us to go blithely on our business all this day, bring us to our resting beds weary and content and undishonored, and grant us in the end the gift of sleep.

You Are What You Think

An unknown author once wrote that "An optimist is a lady who fell out of the 20th story window of a skyscraper and as she passed the fourth floor she said, 'So far, so good.'"

Positive thinking won't prevent the woman from hitting the ground. But researchers are continuing to prove that your thoughts, your emotions, and even your relationships have a great effect on your health and well being. Your positive thoughts actually transform themselves into "chemical entities" like hormones and neurotransmitters that have a direct positive effect on how strong and healthy you feel. Meditation and relaxation techniques not only relieve the short-term stresses you feel, but they also contribute to strengthening your immune system and your ability to fight diseases and long-term stress syndromes.

Our own research in the area of biofeedback and stress management shows conclusively that as people think, so are they. When you think negatively, angrily, and with self-defeating thoughts, your breathing, heart rate, skin response, and brain waves change and put a tremendous strain on your body and mind. When you relax and think positive thoughts, the physiological parameters also calm down and you feel better and more hopeful.

Here is an experience with which you may be able to identify. At your place of employment, due to a malfunctioning computer program, you were not ready to distribute payroll checks at the customary 4 p.m. meeting. Even after fixing the problem and missing the payroll distribution time period by only an hour, your boss seems more irritated than usual. You drive home not only quite tired, but a little disappointed. Upon entering your house you notice an envelope from the IRS. You quickly open the envelope and find a tax refund of $8,000. You can hardly believe it and immediately become energized and excited.

Have you had a similar experience, where you are tired but all of a sudden something very positive happens that causes you to forget your tiredness and to revel in excitement? That's the effect that we're talking about. It comes from something that causes us to think happily and optimistically. We change the chemical activity of our bodies and become more positive people. We are truly what we think. You may not be able to "think and grow rich," like a popular book title suggests, but you can think positively and grow stronger physically and be a happier, more radiant person.

Relationships have a potentially powerful effect on how you

feel. If you're married, you should create a warm personal relationship with your spouse. If you don't have a spouse, find some close personal friends. Most human beings crave intimacy and a sense of community. Nurture yourself socially, and the chances are that you will be a happier and healthier person.

To think positively is to believe that the world is basically a friendly place, that your life is not being threatened by invisible forces, and that there is a reason to feel optimistic.

Develop Your Inner Moral Strength

Much of the anxiety that people experience is self-induced by violations of their own personal code of ethics. When you do things that are in conflict with your core values, you experience considerable stress, deep regret, and, frequently, ill health.

Mitt Romney, former Governor of Massachusetts and founder of a private business, explains the connection between your own personal success, happiness, and living with integrity to your highest values:

> Some years ago, the firm I founded seemed to be coming apart at the seams. Our five partners were at each other's throats. It seemed we all wanted different things from our lives and from our business. One was consumed with making money; he was obsessed with becoming a member of the Forbes 400. Another wanted power and control. I was of two minds, trying to balance the goals of my faith with the money I was earning. We met with a team-building consultant-psychologist. At the end of our week-long session, he led us to something transforming.

Romney said that if we lived our lives in conflict with our core values, we would experience stress, ill health, and deep regret. How, we asked, could we know what our core values were? He asked the audience to think of the five or six people they most admired and respected — people currently living or who had ever lived. Then he asked them to write down next to each of those names the five or six attributes they thought of when they thought of that person. The attributes listed most frequently, he explained, represented core values. Quite simply, if we live in concert with those values, we live with integrity. We would be happy and fulfilled. And, in contrast, if we live in a way that was not consistent with those core values, we ultimately will be unfulfilled and unhappy.

With these values at the our center, chance does not come into play in determining our success or failure. The ability to live with integrity is entirely up to us. Fundamentally, this is the business of successful living.

If you are trying to enhance your feelings of happiness and you want to strengthen yourself inwardly as well as outwardly or physically, you must first identify your core values and then decide whether you are living your life in concert and consistent with those core values.

Determine Your Core Values

To determine your core values, think of five people you most admire and respect. These can be people who are living or who have lived.

List these five people in the spaces numbered 1 through 5.

1. _____

    a. _____

    b. _____

    c. _____

    d. _____

2. _____

    a. _____

    b. _____

    c. _____

    d. _____

3. _____

    a. _____

    b. _____

    c. _____

    d. _____

4. _____

    a. _____

    b. _____

    c. _____

    d. _____

5. _____

    a. _____

    b. _____

c. _____

d. _____

Don't go any further until you have written five names on the 1 through 5 lines above. This is an important exercise because sometimes we experience inner anxiety because we are in conflict with a personal value that we have not clearly identified. When you have identified five people that you admire, go back and write down under each name (a through d) the four attributes that you think of with regards to that person.

When you have filled in all the "a to d" lines with attributes, review what you have written and select the attributes that appear most frequently. Write these on the lines below, as they represent some of your most obvious core values:

_____

_____

_____

_____

_____

The questions you need to ask yourself at this point are, "Do I live in harmony with these core values?" "Do I make decisions that are in concert with my core values?" If you experience discomfort, unhappiness, and a feeling of being unfulfilled, you may want to examine whether you are acting in a way that is consistent with your core values. You cannot reduce the anxious feeling until you fix the cause.

Secret #5   106

Embrace the Tranquil Way

Acapulco, just like the ads say, is a world-renowned synonym for relaxation and fun. Located on the Pacific Coast of Mexico, it really is an almost perfect climate and place for all kinds of relaxation, day and night.

A group of us had come to Acapulco to present a research paper but mostly to get away from the daily routine of university activities and to enjoy ourselves. As we piled out of the taxi in front of the stately and elegant hotel, we were ready for a little relaxation and fun. Little did we realize that we were about to learn a significant lesson about what to do when we are feeling a little stressed and overwhelmed with all the activities inherent in daily living.

This particular hotel is located in the heart of what is known as the "golden zone" of Acapulco and on Condesa Beach. On one side there are shops, night clubs, and restaurants that extend to Acapulco's world-famous La Quebrada, where divers jump alone and in pairs from 136-foot rocky cliffs to the churning surf below. On the other side is a colorful spectacle of hotels and beaches where tourists parasail, jet ski, and wind surf. Off in the distance, you can see the Sierra Madre Mountains, tropical jungles, and some almost hidden lagoons. It is awesome, to say the least.

We carried and pulled our luggage inside the hotel's spacious entry and presented ourselves to the check-in clerk. Each couple was assigned a room and given a key. We and our spouses were assigned rooms, but were told that no keys were available, although one would be made shortly. We were further instructed that on the seventh floor, where our rooms were located, there would be a maid on duty and she would open the rooms for us.

We shuffled off to the seventh floor, found the maid, and unloaded our suitcases into the closets and drawers. The view was spectacular, only now looking down instead of up, along the line of exotic hotels, each with a swimming pool and within a stone's throw of the sandy beach and ocean.

As the evening approached, our group decided that it would walk around a little, find a not-too-expensive restaurant, and eat dinner. The food was good, the tasty fruit drinks were superb (don't ever drink unbottled water unless you want to become acquainted with "Montezuma's Revenge"), and the conversation was relaxed and delightful.

At the end of the meal, the waiter presented us with the bill. A colleague, who's mind operates a little faster than a speeding bullet, looked at the bill, translated everything into American dollars, and realized that there was an error. He called the waiter back, and pointed out the error. "No problem," said the waiter. "We fix you up." The waiter then left our view for a few minutes, returned, and presented the slightly altered bill to my colleague.

The bill was still incorrect. Again, the bill was handed to the waiter who looked at it and asked, "What should the bill be?" My colleague pointed out the error. The waiter's response was, "Don't worry about it. We fix you up." Only this time the waiter walked a few steps away from the table, changed the bill to what he was informed it should be, stepped back to the table and said, "See, I tole you; we fix you up!"

We all had a good laugh, gave a little extra tip to the waiter, and walked back to our hotel. We approached the desk clerk and asked for our keys. He told us that they hadn't been able to make the keys yet, but "Don't worry about it, we will get one for you." We commented how similar the clerk and the waiter's response had been.

We stayed in Acapulco for four days and three nights. Each day we'd ask for our keys and we were given several versions of, "Don't worry about it, we fix you up." Sometimes the clerk was a man, sometimes a woman, and, on several occasions, a very young person. It didn't matter who was tending the counter, they all spoke the same language: "Don't worry about it, we fix you up."

We did receive keys to our rooms the night before we were scheduled to leave. By this time we had learned a couple of things: The maid on the seventh floor who kept unlocking our room for us was a nice person. We also learned from our Acapulco experience that it was quite OK to say, "Don't worry about it, we fix you up."

We returned to the University and walked into the main office on Monday morning. Several secretaries hit us with a load of phone calls that had to be returned and a number of people that we needed to see. You could identify every person who had been to Acapulco. Deluged with a pile of things that had to be done now, each person continued to walk leisurely through the office and quietly said, "Don't worry about it, we fix you up!"

Do You Embrace Tranquility?

Let's face it: We live in a hectic and demanding world. Adversity and conflict seem to surround us on every side. People make insensitive comments about us. How do you respond when you hear such negative comments? Frequently, defective computers, household appliances, cars, lawnmowers and almost everything mechanical and electrical break down. All of this adds to our daily woes and becomes a regular source of irritation.

Everyday you see people who are upset and anxious by what the government is doing, how a neighbor is acting, or what new law is being passed. You can become depressed because it's a cold, rainy day instead of a sunny one, or because it's winter rather than summer. When you react to people and things around you and let them dictate how you feel, you realize that you're living life on an emotional roller coaster. One hour you're up and happy, the next you're down and discouraged. To allow other things and people to irk and vex you is to give them control of your life.

The point that we are trying to make is that these frustrating stressors are not going to go away. In fact, these kinds of irritations may be a part of your daily environment. Consider the following directions from rather disparate sources as to how to cope successfully with the relentless force of these negative events:

> "Master, how may I walk a peaceful path when the world is seldom peaceful?"
>
> "Peace lies not in the world, Grasshopper, but in the man who walks the path."
>
> *—From "Kung Fu"*

In other words, if we look for happiness and peace in the world, we may never find it.

Also consider the comments of University of Chicago Professor Mihaly Csikszentmihalyi, which were made at the Leisure and Mental Health Conference in Salt Lake City, Utah, on July 9, 1992:

> What I discovered was that happiness is not something that happens. It is not the result of good fortune or random change. It is not something that money can buy or power command. It does not depend on outside events, but, rather, on how we interpret them. Happiness, in fact, is a condition that must be prepared for, cultivated, and defended privately by each person. People who learn to control inner experience will be able to determine the quality of their lives, which is as close as any of us can come to being happy.

So here we have two sources explaining how to begin to embrace a more tranquil way of living. One direction is given almost poetically from the ancient Shao Lin Temple Priest, and the other from a contemporary cognitive scientist. But both suggest that we must make an effort to change the way we react to the world if we want to secure for ourselves a more peaceful and tranquil life. We will never be able to control everything in the world around us, but we can control how we react to it and, thus, begin to live life more confidently and tranquilly.

The following quiz will give you a pretty good idea where you are in terms of living your life in a more tranquil way. Be sure to circle your response with a pencil or pen so that you can add up your score and interpret it.

THE TRANQUILITY QUIZ

F = Frequently	0 = Occasionally	N = Not Usually

1. I avoid becoming angry when things do not go my way.   F O N

2. I begin the morning with a soothing shower and a leisurely period of getting dressed.   F O N

3. I focus on results rather than distractions.   F O N

4. I avoid reacting to others with bitterness and resentment.   F O N

5. I avoid becoming irritated by defective appliances, tools, noisy people and a car that malfunctions when I need it most.   F O N

6. I relax, take deep breaths, and stay calm when others disturb me.   F O N

7. I react with emotional resilience when trouble develops.   F O N

8. I avoid being a "moody person."   F O N

9. I also avoid worrying about and regretting my past.   F O N

10. I leave for work early.   F O N

Give yourself 3 points for each "F" score, 2 points for each "O" score, and 1 point for each "N" score. Now total the scores.

A score of 25 to 30 points indicates that you are making a strong effort to embrace a tranquil way of living and have already achieved some success. Keep reading this chapter for more suggestions on how to keep moving ahead in your quest.

A score of 19 to 24 indicates that you are headed in the right direction but need to sharpen up in a few areas. See if you can ultimately push some of the Occasional scores into the Frequently column.

A score of 18 or fewer suggests that you are not doing as well as you could be. Give yourself credit for what you are doing but consider some changes in the way you live your life so as to encompass more of the Frequently scores.

Start the Morning Peacefully

In a recent issue of *Fast Company* magazine, Ben Carson, pediatric neurosurgeon at John Hopkins Children Center in Baltimore, Maryland, said,

> I have found that having a morning ritual — meditation or some quiet reading time — can set the tone for the whole day. Every morning, I spend a half-hour reading the Bible, especially the Book of Proverbs. There's so much wisdom there. During the day, if I encounter a frustrating situation, I think back to one of the verses that I read that morning. Take *Proverbs 16:32,* for example: "He that is slow to anger is better than the mighty, and he who rules his spirit than he who takes a city."

Most people find that to embrace a more tranquil way of living and walk a more peaceful path during the day, they must allow more time than usual to get up and get ready for the activities of the day. This may mean getting up 20 to 30 minutes earlier, but it is well worth it.

Remember our previous illustration from a Mission Bay seminar where we learned how to feel a cool drink of water move refreshingly down our throats and energizing our whole bodies? When was the last time you got up early enough to enjoy a warm soothing shower? Did you feel the water on your neck and back?

Did you have enough time to stand quietly for a few minutes with your eyes closed, caressed by a good feeling, and totally relaxed? And then did you have plenty of time to casually dry yourself, appreciate the newness of the day, and find something appropriate and comfortable to wear?

An important key here is to follow Peter Ducker's advice and allow more time than what these tasks usually take. Don't start the day behind time. Relax into the day. Stay in complete control of this most exhilarating time of the day. Embracing the tranquil way starts with peace, not anxiety. Fears of being late to an appointment or getting behind are not compatible with living a peaceful life. Remember, you get to decide. It's your choice. Make a decision that favors less anxiety and more peacefulness.

By the way, most highly anxious and stressed people do not allow themselves enough time to take a shower, groom themselves properly, and eat a nourishing breakfast. They ignore the very things that reduce anxiety and stress. These same overly stressed people generally grab a cup of coffee or a caffeine laden soda pop in the morning and usually end up skipping lunch. By the time they return home from work, they are generally ready to collapse into bed rather than look forward to a great time with their spouse and family or working on a personal hobby or project.

As we learn from Ben Carson, morning is a great time to pray, to meditate, to think about the good things in life, and to listen to your inner thoughts and directions. Some people find it helpful to read their favorite biblical passages or other positive messages. People of the Christian faith are quick to notice that Jesus is a good example of a person who didn't become overly anxious in the presence of storms at sea or persecutions from fellow citizens of the Roman Empire. Reading about heroic actions in the face of much adversity gives us hope that we can also be a hero in facing our own personal challenges.

As W. C Fields once said, "Start off everyday with a smile and get it over with."

Create a Ritual

Many of our friends play up-beat or inspirational music as they start their day or get ready to go to work. Whatever you do, if it works successfully for you, turn it into a ritual and do it every day. For most of us, that is the only way we can make sure to do things that relax us and energize us on a regular basis. You must separate and protect certain bits of time in your life and choose how you will use them. If you don't make some decisions about your morning time, somebody else will.

If you have to drive to work each day, leave early enough so that you don't have to rush and panic because of heavy traffic or unexpected delays. If you have time to relax as you drive, listen to some music, and notice the beautiful scenery along the way; you may even enjoy the trip and get to work considerably less stressed.

Sometimes we are so stressed at the beginning of our day that we don't even notice how blue the sky is or where the clouds are or the refreshing cool morning breeze. In winter-cold weather, many of us are afraid to breathe in the cold air, which can make us feel more alive and awake. We often treat cool rain in the same manner. We avoid it, preferring to stay inside, huddling and drinking hot chocolate. These might be good times to do just the opposite. How about running outside in the rain or the snow, feeling it fall against your face, getting wet? By the way, if you have kids, they will think you are the absolutely coolest mom or dad that ever existed.

Don't Let People and Things Control You

Several years ago we were sitting in the living room of some friends in California. The morning was beautiful. The sun was shining and the refreshing ocean breeze was pushing its way through the house. Suddenly, the mother jumped up from her chair, pointed out the widow, and said, "Look at that. Do you see what that lady is doing?" We quickly congregated around the window and saw a neighbor lady out walking her dog. "I just know that lady is going to let her dog mess on my lawn."

Actually, the neighbor lady had a pretty tight leash on her dog and the dog did not mess on our friend's lawn. But the mother was almost traumatized by the neighbor lady and her dog. She spent the next few minutes clearly irritated and explaining all the faults of her neighbors. What started out as a calm discussion with a rather peaceful individual had suddenly turned into a serious interruption of our conversation and a major disturbance in her previously calm disposition.

How many times has someone said something to you by way of judgment or rejection, or made a negative comment about what you did or an idea that you had? How did you feel? Did you feel angry or depressed? How do you respond, for example, when you have a flat tire on the way to work? Or what happens inside of you when your computer stops functioning in the middle of an important task?

We live in a world of people, things, and processes. People are sometimes mean and unthinking. They say and do things that undermine us and our happiness. If you feel rather happy and then feel sad because of what someone else says or does, you give away control of your feelings. You let someone else decide how you are going to feel.

Things frequently don't function properly, even things like a neighborhood meeting or a business party. If you let everything that malfunctions make you angry or distressed, you have just turned over the control of your feelings to an inhuman, insensitive, non-thinking, and non-feeling object.

Think about it. Do you really want to let an inanimate object or another human being control the way you feel? Of course you don't. Getting irrational and angry over a thing that malfunctions or a person that makes disparaging judgments about you may not be the most positive or sensible way to respond. You, not things, are in control. You, not people that engage in unkind acts, should stay in control.

You have the power to chart your course and control your mind. That power comes from positively interpreting outside events, learning to control the inner experience, and determining your own response to what is happening around you. You can and must determine how you will respond; you cannot afford to just react. You can't control the world around you, but you certainly can control the way you respond to the world around you.

A Four-Action Plan

Listed below are four powerful actions that will help keep you calm and in control when you are confronted by a potentially irritating experience.

1. Zip Your Lip

Your mouth gets you into more trouble than any of your other parts. When you are nervous and upset, you tend to say things and do things that you regret at a later time. Too often you become defensive and fire back a message that only makes the whole situation worse. Or you start venting your frustrations on an inanimate object, which simply adds to the intensity of your upset feelings.

The psychological admonition is that negative verbalizing does little to relieve your frustrations and anxieties. The biblical admonition from *Proverbs 21:24* is that "Whoso keepeth his mouth and his tongue keepeth his soul from troubles." Zipping the lip gives you time to avoid a negative conditioned response and to figure out how to respond in a more positive and useful way. When confronted with an upsetting situation, zipping the lip is actually the simplest and quickest thing you can do to stay in control.

2. Take Some Deep Breaths and Relax

The onset of any emotional disturbance causes your body to tense up. The nature of an emotion is to come on quickly and stay as long as you allow it to stay. With negative and disturbing feelings, you are particularly vulnerable to losing your confidence and surrendering to feelings of fear and anxiety. You must act immediately to ameliorate those emotional feelings before they totally destroy your efforts to stay peaceful and tranquil.

For many years, stress management experts have been aware of the benefits of deep breathing. Just a few breaths can relieve a tremendous amount of tension and enable you to respond more favorably to a disturbing event. Also, if you breathe through your nose, you breathe slower and deeper. As we suggested before, during mini-breaks don't breathe up and down, breathe from your belly like a baby. If you breathe properly, you will breathe in and out rather than lifting your chest up and down.

You may want to practice deep breathing before you experience a stressful situation. If you're in a position to do so, take the time right now to lie down on the floor. Place your hand on your belly and breathe. From the prone position, it is quite easy to breathe in a way that is relaxing to the whole body. You'll feel your belly rise and fall with each breath. This is what we call belly breathing or breathing like a baby. Try to relax your whole body while you slowly breathe in and out through your nose. With a little practice you will be able to belly breathe standing up and quickly feel a relaxing response take place within your body.

As Hindu monk Vivekananda advised, "It is the greatest manifestation of power to be calm."

3. Think a Peaceful Thought

Think about how good it feels to be on the peaceful path and embrace a more tranquil way of living. Tell yourself that you would prefer to stay on it rather than fall off. This simply means to really relax, fill yourself with the images of the magnificent wonders and opportunities that surround you. See the great gifts, talents, and potential in others.

To think a peaceful thought, you may want to recall a lovely place on a warm beach or in the cool mountains that you have enjoyed. Picture yourself in such a relaxing place. Immerse yourself in the scene: Feel it, see it, and enjoy it. Imagining a tranquil scene or experience tends to relax your mind and body. With a little practice, thinking a peaceful thought can have an immediate and profound effect on calming you down so that you can control your feelings.

If you let another person or thing irritate you, the situation will be like putting a little stone in front of your eye. The stone is so close to your eye that you cannot see anything else. To stay in control and continue in a tranquil way, you need to focus on the bigger picture or on a specific comfortable and soothing thought. This way, you can stay in control and relax.

Imagine yourself confronted by an individual who tells you, "That was the stupidest damn thing that I have ever seen you do!" If you're a normal, sensitive human being, your first response will be one of irritation, surprise, and a strong sense of urgency to retaliate in some way. However, before you attack, recount what you've just learned. First, delay responding immediately and avoid calling the other person names that refer to their illegitimate birth or the malfunctioning of their brain. Don't make any kind of spontaneous verbal response, which only aggravates matters more and upsets you further. Just zip your lip. Don't say anything. This may unnerve your adversaries, but, so what, that's their problem, not yours.

Now breathe. Just take a few deep breaths and relax. Don't make this too obvious to the others involved. They will be somewhat surprised that you haven't said anything yet. They may come totally unglued when you hold your ground and simply look at them and breathe. At any rate, if you've done steps one and two, you will be ready for step three: to think a peaceful thought.

Let your mind quickly engage in a peaceful thought. Take a two-second trip to Maui, Hawaii, and once again feel the warm breeze, sandy beach, and slow run of the surf. Remember, the mind directly affects the body. Think a peaceful thought and the whole body tends to become peaceful. With a little practice these first three steps can be done in fewer than five seconds, which is enough time to totally confuse your neighbor or some other irritant.

4. Decide What Kind of Response Is Necessary

This is the golden moment. You are calm and in control. You haven't relegated your feelings to someone else or to some inanimate object. You have avoided making an unthinking, irresponsible response. You are not yelling or screaming back at someone or something. Your breathing is normal and you have just revisited a moment of warmth and relaxation. Now you are ready to decide what to say and do.

As with the washing machine, you may just want to respond with a good laugh and call a repairman. With a person, you may decide that the most appropriate response is no response. You may decide to just walk away, whistle a happy tune, and forget it. Or, you may feel so good that you tell the other person that you didn't know they would be so upset with what you did and simply say, "I'm sorry. I didn't know this was happening. How can we make things better?"

Obviously, if you are the object of a harsh judgment by another person, you need to listen carefully and decide whether it's accurate or a simple misperception. In any case, remaining calm allows you to approach the situation in a way that opens the gate for you and the other person to seek more comfortable understanding and find a peaceful solution. The eye-for-an-eye and a bunch-of-teeth-for-a-tooth approach is unproductive for embracing the tranquil way.

Resentment and Regret: Twin Enemies

Staying peaceful when the whole world around you seems to be falling apart is one of the most difficult tasks in the world. You can, however, stay strong and in control by following the four powerful steps that we have just explained. These four actions pretty much neutralize the negative edge of people and things. Since people and things are external to you or outside of you, you can just take control of your feelings and choose the tranquil way.

Resentment

On the other hand, resentments that you hold toward people who seem to consciously or deliberately threaten you in some way create pain inside of you. Furthermore, if you carry bitterness and resentment because of what someone did or said to you in the past, you can expect to have an equally large amount of pain. If you carry resentment and bitterness within, you have decided to live with a certain amount of emotional pain. You'll find it difficult to feel tranquil when you're feeling angry and hateful.

The fact is that even if another person has tried to hurt you deliberately, it is your own negative feelings, not the other person's attempt to hurt you, that produce pain in your life. The other person may be sun bathing on the beach, enjoying life. You are the one paying a terrible price for allowing yourself to feel bitterness, hate, malice, and resentment.

So you have to decide. If your own negative feelings are the problem, how long are you going to allow yourself to feel upset, irritated, and disgruntled? You're the only one who can make this decision. No one else in the whole world knows specifically what you're feeling inside, and no one else in the whole world can make that decision for you.

Regret

Another challenge to your inner peace and tranquility comes about when you regret and dwell on the mistakes that you have made in the past. All of us make mistakes and all of us have regrets about some acts we performed or failed to perform in the past. This book is too short to list all the dumb things that we shouldn't have done, especially during our early lives.

But when you dwell on the regrets of the past, this will disturb your ability to embrace the tranquil way. For example, a number of years ago an attractive woman went to obtain some counseling from her ecclesiastical leader. She was about 55 years old, carried herself well, and seemed very polite. Her religious leader happened to be a friend of ours and renowned for his easy manner and great counseling skills. He reported later that the woman spent about 30-minutes telling him about a past act that she was still regretting. She was filled with sorrow and remorse and cried frequently during their visit.

He told us that "this fine woman allowed herself to be tormented and filled with regret for a single act that took place thirty years ago!" He was able to help her appreciate that she was now living a good and honorable life and that the past act was only a singular act for which she had truly made the proper restitution.

You can more fully embrace the tranquil life if you stop resenting and regretting things that took place yesterday, and the day before and the past. If you can repair a past error, then go ahead and do it. If you resent some unkind or thoughtless person, forget it and move on with your life. Resenting an unkind word will not change the word. But forgetting the word or the thoughtless act does change you and how you feel.

The real lesson to be learned from the past and the future is this: Don't regret and dwell on the past, learn from the past. Don't worry about the future, plan for the future. Enjoy the present. Embrace the moment. Breathe and live. Don't regret and worry. You have nothing to lose and everything to gain by living in the fullest possible way now. Consider that the darkness of the past pales in the sunshine of today. As far as tomorrow is concerned, what could you do better than live well today?

Reconnect With Your Spirituality

We were presenting a seminar on the subject of "Revitalizing Yourself." After talking about various ways to re-energize ourselves on a daily basis, we asked the audience a rather simple question: "How many in this audience believe that when you die, that is the end of yourself? You will cease to exist as any kind of individual identity? If you believe that, please raise your hand."

Not a single hand was raised among the 300 people attending this particular seminar. We ventured another question to the audience, "What do you call the part of you that doesn't follow your body into the grave?"

The audience responded with these answers:

My spiritual essence
My soul
My spirit
My eternal self

The real me
The one who's thinking and talking right now

These findings are confirmed by Gallup polls, which show that 96% of Americans are religious believers and only 4% define themselves as atheists or agnostics. Since the down turn in the economy, the increase in financial worries, along with worries of terrorism and impending war with countries that violate arms pacts, more people are turning to religion and various spiritual support groups for help. Our seminar attendees tell us that they seek spirituality "to feel balanced and grounded," "gain confidence to do things," and "to fight off the negative, and "to feel more peace within myself."

What Is Spirituality?

A survey completed by *Self* magazine that appeared in the December 1997 issue asked respondents to define spirituality. Some popular responses were: "Connection to a reality that is more than self and comforts and guides us," "Belief in a higher power," "A connection to all living things and to the Earth and universe," and "A close personal relationship with God." This survey also reported that 93% of the respondents believed that having a spiritual life is important, and 88% reported that they believed in a supreme being.

The reasons for having a spiritual life were similar to the responses from our own workshop audiences: "to attract positive situations and people," "to feel at peace with myself and cope with stress"and "We are three-dimensional beings — physical, emotional, and spiritual."

Most of us feel that we are more than physical entities, and that we have another part that doesn't die when our body dies. We frequently refer to that part as the spiritual side of ourselves. It also is quite clear that we need to strengthen and embrace that spiritual side if we are to find deep inner power and tranquility. True inner peace may elude us if we neglect one of the most important and yet hidden parts of ourselves — the soul.

How Do You Begin?

A look at new books for sale reveals a deluge of treatises dealing with spirituality and religion. Everything from *Conversations with God* to *The Ten Challenges* now graces our bookshelves. New Age authors encourage us to explore everything from pyramid power to the spiritual traditions of Native Americans, and alternative spirituality advocates take us to reports from nearly dead people to Virgin Mary sightings. Since having a strong faith or belief in something seems to be such an important part of embracing a more peaceful and tranquil way of living, we would like to make some suggestions about how to begin your search.

1. Re-examine Your Spiritual Tradition

Before you change from your childhood religion, or start out on the search for a new faith, examine the traditions of your present religious faith. You may find that you weren't even aware of some of its strongest tenets. Those who have been reared in Judaism or Christianity may find great strength in the Jewish and Christian scriptures. For many, The Ten Commandments provide enduring wisdom and a strong foundation for their faith.

2. Look for the Strong Points

You are not alone in your search, so be open to insights from where ever they may come to you. Other people may have found a direction that will also work for you. Listen to what they're saying. Therapy groups, various programs for addiction, and various religious services have been known to awaken or rekindle a spiritual life in those who are looking. You don't have to make an immediate decision to join any of them in your quest, but do see if the values they cherish are what you are looking for.

If you do join a religious community of some kind, and you participate actively in that religious group, you will receive support from its members, and guidance from its leaders. Trying to face the challenges of daily living is a huge task when you try to do it alone. Having the support of a religious group provides a dependable form of support and comfort, especially when you face personal disasters and defeats.

If your present faith seems like it is not helping, then go find a better teacher or mentor. Re-read the basic texts associated with your present faith to deepen your understanding of what you have, before you embark on a new search; however, continue searching until you find a community that feels right and offers you the spiritual strength you need.

3. Meditate or Pray

Set aside time each day to pray or meditate. Quietly meditating and going to the stillness within may give you sudden strokes of insight as to the meaning of life. Herbert Benson, M.D., associate professor of medicine at Harvard University's Medical School in Boston and author of *The Relaxation Response*, says that to maximize your prayer time, you should learn how to relax into prayer. He suggests an approach quite similar to what we have described earlier in this book: get comfortable, breathe steadily, focus on a word or phrase, preferably from your religious faith, and look inward, contemplate your faith, and experience a feeling of peace.

Set aside time in the morning, afternoon or evening, to pray, meditate, or to follow the disciplines of yoga or tai chi. Spend time finding inner stillness through reading great literature or by calming your body and spirit. You may want to devise your own rituals. In any case, do something that reminds you of your great blessings, and connects you more closely with good people and sound values.

4. Give someone a Helping Hand

Nobel Prize winner Albert Schweitzer once said, "Do something for somebody every day for which you do not get paid."

This is good advice. One of the quickest ways to feel strong spiritually is to quit focusing on yourself and do something for someone else. The more valuable the action is — and the more time and resources it takes — the better you feel. This is another reason to join a spiritual community. It draws us out of ourselves. As a member of one of these groups, you are reminded frequently to help others, and you will be given the opportunity to do so.

One of the most common phrases heard today is "unconditional love." The words come easily in conversations about how we should relate to people who have messed up their lives: "Show unconditional love to everyone, God does it." Too often, however, unconditional love for all humanity emphasizes self, rather than others. We feel good by believing that we possess unconditional love. Nevertheless, we don't engage others in a real demonstration of love, especially with our neighbors and community members.

Stepping Onto the Tranquil Path

Embracing the tranquil way is a process rather than an act. To begin this process, step forward and start the morning peacefully. Then turn whatever you do to start the morning peacefully into a ritual and do it every day. Avoid allowing people and things to control you because you have the power to chart your own course and control your mind. That power comes from positively interpreting outside events. Control your inner experience, and determine your own responses to what is happening around you.

Be sure to implement these four powerful suggestions for sustaining yourself in a tranquil way when something irritating happens to you: zip your lip, take some deep breaths and relax, think a peaceful thought, and decide what kind of response is necessary.

Resentment and regret are twin enemies of the tranquil way. Cast off the past, plan for the future, but do learn to enjoy the present by embracing the moment. Reconnect with your spirituality and use the power of your faith. Re-examine the spiritual tradition most familiar to you by looking for its strong points, then meditate or pray for inspiration. Finally, give someone a helping hand. The gift of giving reinforces your pursuit of the tranquil way.

Concerning this last point, a significant amount of research reveals that older adults who give emotional and practical help tend to live longer than those who focus on getting help. Studies at the University of Michigan, the University of California at Los Angeles, and Arizona State University confirm the findings that giving day-to-day help protects the helper's health. Even though giving tends to prolong life, the primary benefit for you is a more tranquil and peaceful existence right now, today.

Seize the Moment

7

We, like you, have looked around our own neighborhood and found too many people who seem to be overwhelmed with the demands of daily living. In fact, we have had the additional opportunity to observe hundreds of people in seminars who are nurturing tremendous amounts of anxiety and discouragement because they don't understand how to make their lives more peaceful and prosperous.

The irony of this whole mess is that being more effective and peaceful is not a function of how hard one works, how hard one tries, or how intelligent and knowledgeable a person is. Being more successful and happy is something apart from all of that. It consists of doing correct and rather simple things like those we have been explaining in this book.

For most of us it means discarding some of the practices and behaviors of the past and trying something new — in short, being malleable and teachable. Lao-Tzu, the father of Taoism, put it this way:

The Way of Life

A man is born gentle and weak.
At his death he is hard and stiff.
Green plants are tender and filled with sap.
At their death they are withered and dry.
Therefore the stiff and unbending
is the disciple of death.
The gentle and yielding is the disciple of life.
Thus an army without flexibility never wins a battle.
A tree that is unbending is easily broken.
The hard and the strong will fall.
The soft and weak will overcome.

Being teachable and flexible also means that we must stop carrying the frustrations of the past and open up ourselves to new experiences and new ways to live our lives. Consider this Zen story.

The Muddy Road

Two monks were walking along a muddy road when they came upon a beautiful woman unable to cross the road without getting her silk shoes muddy. Without saying a word, the first monk picked up and carried the woman across the road, leaving her on the other side.

Then the two monks continued walking without talking until the end of the day. When they reached their destination, the second monk said, "You know, monks are to avoid women. Why did you pick up that woman this morning?" The first monk replied, "I left her on the side of the road. Are you still carrying her?"

Three Traits of Successful People

Most people who have been able to change their lives for the better have some common traits that enable them to succeed in reaching their goals. We are about to help you develop a plan to drop off some of the feelings and practices that may have kept you from reaching your potential as a successful and happy person. It is imperative for you to realize that disregarding any of the following three traits of successful people will slow you down in achieving your own dream of a happier life.

Be Persistent

No one succeeds at anything with a "hit and miss approach." Doing something now and then is not good enough for you to achieve your goal of simplifying your life and finding ways to live more effectively. Once you start, you must be consistent in your efforts. Do you recall the story of the tortoise and the hare? Occasional bursts of speed are good — if you continue to move ahead steadily in between those short extra bursts of speed. Former President Calvin Coolidge put it this way:

> Nothing in the world can take the place of persistence. Talent will not; nothing is more common than unsuccessful men with talent. Genius will not; unrewarded genius is almost a proverb. Education will not; the world is full of educated derelicts. Persistence and determination alone are omnipotent. The slogan, "press on," has solved and always will solve the problems of the human race.

Few examples illustrate the value of persistence more effectively than the following sequence of events in a certain man's life. His age at the time of each event is recorded.

Incident	Age
Failed in business	22
Defeated for legislature	23
Failed in business, again	24
Elected to legislature	25
Sweetheart died	26
Had nervous breakdown	27
Defeated for speaker of house	29
Defeated for elector	31
Defeated for congress	34
Elected to Congress	37
Defeated for Congress	39
Defeated for Senate	46
Defeated for vice president	47
Defeated for Senate	49
Elected President of the U.S.	51

The person, of course, is Abraham Lincoln.

Believe in Yourself

Remember what we said about being your own worst enemy? You must unbridle your thinking. Become passionate about your efforts to change your life into something better than what it is. Dare to dream. See yourself achieving your personal goals and all the rewards that will accrue if you stick with your plan. We suggest that you make a list of benefits that will come as you achieve your goals. Put your list in a prominent place so that you can visualize daily all the wonderful opportunities and values that will be yours as you learn to overcome daily frustrations and learn how to embrace a more tranquil way of living.

An elderly carpenter was ready to retire. He told his employer, a building contractor, about his plans to leave the building business and live a more leisurely life with his spouse and extended family. Although he would miss a regular paycheck, they could get by.

The contractor was sorry to see his good worker go, and asked if he would build just one more house as a personal favor. The carpenter agreed, but in time it was easy to see that his heart was not in his work. He resorted to shoddy workmanship and used inferior materials. It was an unfortunate way to end a dedicated career.

When the carpenter finished his work, the contractor came to inspect the house. He handed the front door key to the carpenter. "This is your house," he said. "My gift to you." The carpenter was shocked. What a shame! If he had only known that he was building his own house, he would have done it differently.

So it is with all of us. We build our lives, one day at a time, failing to believe that we should do the best we can at all times. Then, with a shock, we realize that we must live the life we have constructed. Believe in yourself so as to be passionate about the life you are building and do your very best at all times.

Be Willing to Start Small

Don't use the excuse that small is worthless. It's easy to postpone beginning your quest toward a more sane and peaceful life by thinking that you will be in a better position to start next month or next year. You don't need to be in a better position to get on the road to being a more happy and successful person. In fact, if you start now, you will be amazed at how quickly your small gains and little victories will motivate you to keep going and set even higher goals!

Speaking on the radio years ago, Richard L. Evans, one-time president of Rotary International, explained that the people who have enriched the world the most moved ahead without waiting for ideal conditions to allow them to succeed. They wrote and painted, thought and planned, worked and discovered, often in poverty, illness, or other unsympathetic surroundings. With impelling insight, Evans touched a stinging chord when he stated that "there rarely comes a time in the life of any of us when we cannot find some plausible excuse for not doing something we could or should be doing."

Don't wait, start now — start small, but start. You may think you'll find a more opportune time or mood to proceed to make changes in your life, but you won't. Your habits and your appetites will be just as demanding tomorrow as they are today. Your determination to overcome will be no greater the next day than it is now. Delays in making the decision to begin now may be the delays that steal your own greatness.

Let's Go For A Walk

It is possible to summarize the contents of this book by carefully proceeding from one point to another, logically. Very much like examining a car, we could go to a typical automobile Web site and look at all the statistical data about the dimensions of the car, the performance characteristics, and even compare it with other cars.

Another way to know a car is to walk around it in order to see it from all angles. Sit in it and imagine yourself driving down the road. Start the engine and turn on the radio. Try the heater and see how noisy or quiet the fan is. Take the car for a little test drive.

In the end, a good general view of the car may be obtained that is more real by using a walk around approach than a detailed analysis of the statistical data on the website. In this book we have used a "walk around" approach. We have presented a succession of approaches, stories, images and ideas with the hope that in the end you will have a clear idea of how to triumph in your quest to simplify your life, use your marvelous potentials, and find more success and happiness in meeting the demands of daily living.

When trying to bring a great idea to life by walking around and through it, there is always a certain amount of repetition and overlap present. At times, even some imprecision finds its way into the explanations of various ideas. But that's OK. Your job is to find what works for you. If some approach or idea seems a little defective to you, fix it up — make it right for you. Be creative. Use your smarts and sensitivities to improve upon a good idea. Don't get caught rejecting explanations and gloating over your brilliant analysis because of some past perception you have about what is true or not true, or what works and what doesn't work. That's a waste of psychic energy and none of us have enough to waste.

So, What's The Main Point?

We thought you would never ask. At this point we would like to summarize what we think is the main point of each chapter so that you can get a holistic view of how you become trapped in the demands of daily living and what you can do to get out of the trap and become a more successful and happy person.

Secret 1 — Shift Out of Hyperdrive

You can't do it all. Time is finite but the demands and expectations that are placed upon you and that you place upon yourself are infinite. Something has to give. Hopefully that something won't be your health or well being. You can unburden yourself by using the super sanity model to focus on and resolve those things that are your most irritating concerns at the present time.

Once you start to take care of the things that cause you the most anxiety, you find it easier to handle the rest of your daily activities, and you will find many opportunities to work on your own goals and aspirations. For short term support you should also take mini-relaxation breaks throughout the day. Ultimately you should learn how to relax into everything you do.

Secret 2 — Whistle for Another Lever

You are surrounded by resources that can be of great help in solving your problems and concerns, as well as lightening the burdens of everyday living. Trying to do everything yourself is the most ineffective way to become successful at anything. And for trying to work your way out of feeling overworked and overwhelmed, depending totally on yourself is usually a complete disaster.

Treating others as friends and potential helpers is a good start. Using the "success triangle" is the simplest way to whistle for another lever. Actually, people would like to help you succeed. The problem is that when you are feeling a little discouraged, you frequently don't feel like reaching out for help.

We sometimes cry and share our woes with others, but we don't decide what goal we are trying to achieve and what help we might need to achieve it. The specificity attached to our goals determines who can help us. Using all your resources along with using reliable information helps you accomplish tasks more quickly and dump concerns more efficiently.

Secret 3 — Kick Down the Walls

When taking care of problems and concerns, you don't always have the time, inclination, or skill to analyze all the bits and pieces of the problem and select an appropriate course of action. But you know that the quicker and more effectively you deal with a concern, the quicker you will reduce your stress and anxiety levels. To unleash your creative potential, use the Back to the Future Approach, The Two Question Approach, or the Intuition and Inspiration Approach.

The excitement inherent in being creative and kicking down a few restrictive ways of thinking enables you to eliminate considerable amounts of boredom and anxiety.

Secret 4 — Close Your Company Store

If you want to return to a calmer way of living and find time for yourself, set a "stop time." Setting a stop time is one way to close your company store. A stop time is a time of the day when you stop responding to the events, people, activities and the demands of the day. This is your time to do with it what you want.

Another way to close your company store is to avoid over-planning. Writing down too many appointments and activities puts extraordinary pressure on you to meet those commitments and frequently gets in the way of opportunities to act creatively and spontaneously.

Most people don't know how to calm and quiet themselves so

as to enjoy the various activities of the day. Following the steps outlined in Chapter 4 enables you to relax into everything that you do.

Secret 5 — Grab Your Oxygen First

You can avoid succumbing to the negative effects of the discouragements and burdens that are placed upon you by strengthening yourself physically and morally.

Great physical and mental strength comes from eating the proper foods and avoiding habits that are injurious to your health, such as smoking, drugging, and excessive use of alcohol. Exercising for just 30 minutes a day strengthens your body and your mind. Sleeping well and thinking positive thoughts have enormous energy benefits.

Incredible inner strength comes from living in harmony with your core values. These core values can be determined quite easily by following the "ideal person" exercise. Making judgments that are in harmony with your core values will save you from a lot of useless inner turmoil and will give you amazing inner strength.

Secret 6 — Embrace the Tranquil Way

The world is not peaceful by any means. We can't change the world. The only way we can be tranquil is to control the way we react to the world around us. By remaining calm and in control when confronted by an unthinking person or an irritating mechanical problem is the closest we will ever come to keeping ourselves on the peaceful path. Peacefulness is within us.

It is a lot easier to stay peaceful and in control when you start the morning peacefully. Allowing yourself enough time to groom yourself, eat a good breakfast, listen to some good music, attend to any pressing family matters, depart leisurely, and not rush down the freeway to work are wonderful ways to start and control your day.

When confronted by a frustrating person or situation, the "zip the lip" approach provides the best opportunity to stay calm and react effectively. Paying attention to the spiritual side of yourself is another extremely useful way to find peace, support, and comfort as you make your way through the sometimes stressful terrain of daily life.

Secret 7 — Seize the Moment

The main point of this chapter is to review briefly the other six chapters and devise a plan to make appropriate changes in your life that will bring you greater tranquility, the utmost confidence, and much more personal effectiveness. As with golfing or piano playing, no one becomes an expert simply by reading about it. You have to practice.

To become a more successful and happy person you have to follow the principles suggested in each chapter of this book. As you pick and choose the ideas that work best for you, those ideas become your ideas and become habitual ways for you to think and behave. This book provides you with general coaching in some crucial areas that lead to a more successful and enjoyable way of living your life. But much more important for you is to discover for yourself how to inculcate these powerful ideas into your daily life. Or, conversely, figure out what is keeping you from using these simple ideas to strengthen yourself and enhance your life.

How to Change

Unfortunately, no one is going to improve your life for you. No one is going to wind you up each morning and get you going. No one is going to take responsibility for your personal success. You have to do these things yourself.

A recent report researched the question, "Why don't more things happen in our lives? Why don't we accomplish more?" The answer was startling. The report said that most things fail to happen because there is no plan to make them happen. We thought it might be a lack of motivation or commitment. But no, whether a plan exists or not makes the difference.

We have watched many people succeed. How do they do it? We can tell you that it's not just by waking up every morning with a smile on their face and a winning attitude. It's waking up each morning with a darn good plan for achieving success.

There is nothing that motivates us more than knowing that we have a way to be successful. Success breeds success. One little success leads to another. A wise sage said that, "Inch by inch life's a cinch, yard by yard it's kind of hard." A good plan gets us started, keeps us going, and gives us hope.

As American clergyman Harry Emerson Fosdick noted:

> No steam or gas ever drives anything until it is confined.
> No Niagara is ever turned into light and power until it is tunneled.
> No life ever grows great until it is focused, dedicated, disciplined.

Make Your Plan and Work It

Making a plan is extraordinarily simple and consists of only a few key items. Constructing a plan means figuring out (1) what you want to achieve, (2) when you are going to achieve it, (3) how you are going to achieve it and (4) keeping the rewards and benefits in mind that will accrue to you when you achieve your goal.

1. Set a Goal

This can be done by reviewing the main point of each chapter or by reviewing some of the exercises in each chapter and selecting one or more actions that you would like to do more often. Select those actions that are important to you or those that result in some kind of pain when you fail to do them. Be cautious in trying to change well-entrenched behaviors at the beginning. It may be better to take a goal that seems important but that involves behaviors that you can change somewhat easily. Then you experience immediate success and feel that you can continue to have success in achieving the next goal.

Try also to define your goal in terms of some observable act or behavior. An observable act is one that can be seen by others and is easy to verify. For example, using the "zip your lip" approach when encountering a stressful situation is an observable act. Be specific about your goal and then write it down on a piece of paper as a way of committing yourself to the goal.

2. Set a Date for Achieving Your Goal

Try to be as specific as possible and write the goal achievement date on a piece of paper below your goal. Sometimes you may want to include where, and with whom you will make this change. If you want to "whistle for another lever" and use all the resources that are available to you, you may need to decide where and from whom you will solicit help. The main point is to begin now to implement your changes.

3. Decide How You Will Achieve Your Goal

Be sure that you not only have a specific goal, but that you have a rather specific way to achieve your goal. It's great to decide that you will not try to accomplish too much in a single day, but how will you decide what are the most important things that you should do?

Using the super sanity model in Chapter 1 is a specific way for you to achieve your goal. If you pick a vague, ambiguous goal you will have all kinds of difficulty trying to implement that goal. So, as we have suggested, start with a specific goal, a specific time when the goal is to be achieved, and a specific way to achieve the goal. Specificity in each of these three areas leads to success in achieving your goals.

4. Keep the Benefits in Mind

Imagine the benefits that will accrue as you achieve your goal. Can you even begin to imagine what it would be like not to worry about trying to accomplish everything and actually be more successful by doing less? Or think about how you will feel when you start reclaiming your time and your life by implementing one of the suggestions that you have read about in this book?

Take the time to write down some of the benefits that will accrue to you as you achieve your specific goal. The statements that you write will motivate you when you falter a little in making a beneficial change in the way you live your life.

What Do You Really Need to Change?

This is another planning approach that may help you identify specific changes that you will want to put on top of your priority list.

1. Take a piece of paper and write this sentence: "What I really need in my life right now is more _____."

2. Go back through the ideas presented in this book and see if anything seems to jump out at you. Jot down any ideas that you have. These are probably the most immediate things that seem to get in the way of allowing you to be more relaxed and more effective during the day.

3. Ask your spouse or a close friend to look over your ideas and see if they agree or if they can add anything to what you have written.

4. At this point, make a plan to change these items as quickly as possible using the planning form that we have just suggested. Most people that we consult find this to be a quick way to decide what changes to make first.

Using Mental Imagining

Imaging or using mental practice is one of the single most neglected tools for transforming yourself from where you are now, in terms of the way you confront the challenges of daily living, to where you would like to be. This change process is quite simple to use:

First, write a statement about how you really behave during a day when you feel a little overwhelmed with life. You may want to ask yourself, "How do my fellow employees, associates and family members see me behave when I am a little stressed out during the day?" Their perceptions of how you really behave on a "bad hair day" may be less biased and more accurate than your own.

Second, visualize in your mind what you believe an ideal in control type of person would be like under similar circumstances. What would they do? How would they speak? How would they come across to their associates?

Third, write down a brief description of the ideal person that you visualized.

Fourth, now take one characteristic of this ideal person, close your eyes, relax, and see yourself actually reaching that ideal. How does it feel? Do you feel more relaxed and confident? What steps did you take to reach this ideal? Did you gain something good by taking this action and realizing this ideal?

Fifth, after visualizing and seeing yourself changing into this ideal person, decide two or three things that you are going to do this week to realize your dream. And, this is most important, visualize yourself doing them successfully in your mind before you attempt to do them literally.

You will be amazed at how effective this whole process of visualization and mental practice is as you make changes in the way you attempt to change your life for the better.

Mushin: No Mind

Notice that when someone throws you a ball, without thought, your hands move up and you catch it. Similarly, when driving along in your car and the traffic light turns red, you automatically apply the brakes. You don't think of the dozens of movements involved in just lifting your hands and catching the ball, or in moving your legs and feet and applying the brakes. You just do it without thinking. This is the state of mind that the Japanese refer to as mushin, which means "without a mind." When you are in a state of mushin your actions become unconscious actions and flow freely and naturally. You don't have to think about how you are going to act or react in a given situation.

It is only through practice and more practice that you can do things without conscious effort. For example, if you have decided to make some changes in your life by identifying some correct principles and strategies that we have described in this book, then you must implement those changes into your life on a regular basis. Each time you use a procedure or try a new behavior it slowly becomes more inculcated into your whole being so that pretty soon it is a way of life for you. That is, you don't have to think about it anymore. You have internalized it. Notice what happened to the student in the follow story.

Anciently, if a youngster wished to learn Kung Fu he would have to pledge himself to a master. One of the most important parts of the pledge was a promise not to leave the master until the student had learned and perfected all the requirements for a particular marshal art style. The penalties were severe for a runaway student, sometimes even death.

A popular story is told about a boy who pledged himself to a famous local master and then tried to escape. When the boy entered the school, he found that his training was tedious and hard and the master paid little attention to him. The student served his master and his older classmates. But the student persevered by watching the older classmates and the master and then imitating them by practicing the forms and techniques.

Years passed and the master barely seemed to notice or teach the student. The student kept watching and practicing. Finally, the student became disenchanted with the whole learning process and decided to run away.

The day finally arrived to run away; however, unknown to the student the master had discovered the escape plan. The master decided to invite the student to dinner and test him. If the student failed the test, he would be killed.

During the dinner, the master put a hard pea in his mouth and spit the pea at him. This master was famous for using internal and external power when spitting hard objects from his mouth; if these projectiles hit an eye or a vital cavity in the face, much damage would result.

When the master spit the pea at him the student instantly knew the master was trying to hurt him. Without thinking the student moved his chopsticks and caught the pea in mid air. The student's continuous practice had given him fast enough reactions to catch the pea.

The amazed master saw this and said, "I had never realized that you have such a capability to defend yourself. I can teach you no more; you are free to go at any time." The student suddenly realized how valuable his time and training had been. He immediately threw himself on the floor and asked his master to forgive him and allow him to stay as a student.

This popular story teaches several important lessons. The first is that to learn certain things takes time and perseverance. In the story, the master tested the student with inattention to see whether he cared enough to really learn the secrets of the Master.

Second, the story pointed out the final results of proper training. Though the student was not specifically trained to catch an object with chopsticks, he was able to do it. This kind of spontaneous reaction only comes about with extensive practice.

So it is with the concepts that you have been reading about in this book. They are not fully comprehended and put into practice overnight. However, by implementing some of them as quickly as possible, you can begin to acquire the ability to act and react spontaneously to any situation that you are likely to encounter in your life.

As you implement the concepts in this book, you improve your life and the way that you handle situations of concern and stress. You feel happier and more confident. In fact, you may be surprised at how well you are doing because you actually find yourself accomplishing more, doing less, and feeling pretty good about your life.

A Zen Riddle

One caution before you take flight for the stars. When you think of showing off your newly acquired skills, your self-awareness will interfere with your performance and you will make mistakes. We guarantee it. Do you understand now the meaning of this ancient Zen riddle: "When you seek it, you cannot find it."

Notice how a professional athlete or a great marshal art Master performs. Pro tennis players don't have time to think about how they are going to hit the ball, neither do pro baseball players. Professional piano players simply play without thinking about each key they need to strike. A practiced person senses the situation that they are in and makes an adjustment or response. It's quite automatic, definitely without thinking, that's mushin. That's where you want to be as you follow the suggestions in this text: relaxed, operating within your best self, and enjoying the moment.

Thousands of people have been helped by following these principles and strategies for contending with being overwhelmed by daily living demands. Many other thousands could alleviate their problems and worries but don't take the time to get a little advice and implement an effective plan for changing things for the better in their lives.

Before Arnold Schwarzenegger became governor of California he would arrange his week with events ranging from a trip to Miami for interviews, to Mexico to work on a movie, then to Japan for a film festival, and back to Mexico to continue his movie work. Listen to his secret: "You have got to have fun with the things you do. And you always look forward, visualize the finished product." Notice that even now, Gov. Schwarzenegger still seems to try to have fun doing things, and he definitely is excited about looking forward and visualizing the finished product.

Our hope and best wish is that you will not spend inordinate amounts of time working and worrying about how to get back control of your life and your time. But that you will look forward to a much improved way of living, visualize your final product and have a lot of fun getting to your goals. If you don't do anything else to increase your peace of mind and personal effectiveness, please try at least one suggestion that we have shared with you between the covers of this book.

About the Authors

ERIC STEPHAN is professor emeritus of organizational leadership and strategy at Brigham Young University. He earned a Ph.D. in communication with an emphasis in educational psychology from the University of Utah. He also completed post-doctoral studies in creative problem solving, training and development, biofeedback, hypnosis and psychosomatics.

Dr. Stephan is coauthor of numerous books, including *Powerful Leadership: How to Unleash the Potential in Others and Simplify Your Own Life* (with Wayne Pace), *What Happy Families are Doing, The Perfect Leader, Me Mum Sez: Outrageous Truths About Life & People, Quiz Me, To Lead as Jesus Led, Listening for Understanding, Creative Problem Solving,* and *How Do you Rate With the Opposite Sex?*

He has delivered hundreds of lectures and seminars to business and civic groups on the subject of success and happiness, being overworked and overwhelmed, including the National Association of State Budget Officers, National Parks and Recreational Administrators, Marriott Corporation, IBM, J. R. Simplot Co., Southwest Nursing Association,

Society of Research Administrators, Utah Home Builders Association, Western States Municipal Treasurer's Association, Utah City Manager's Association, Marriott School of Management Business Management Societies, Parker Aerospace Co., and Bonneville Media Corporation.

He enjoys participating in physical fitness programs, studying about the martial arts, ride motorcycles, engage in entrepreneurial enterprises and just relax into life's daily activities. He can be reached at <EricGStephan@gmail.com>.

WAYNE PACE is a Senior Partner in WPC & Associates, a management development consulting firm with offices in Singapore and St. George, Utah. He is also professor emeritus of organizational leadership in the Marriott School of Management at Brigham Young University and has been an adjunct professor in the School of Social and Workplace Development at Southern Cross University, NSW, Australia.

Dr. Pace is author or coauthor of more than 100 articles and nearly two dozen books, including *Organizational Dynamism: Unleashing Power in the Workforce; Powerful Leadership: How to Unleash the Potential in Others and Simplify Your Own Life* (with Eric Stephen)*; Training Across Multiple Locations; Organizational Communication; Human Resource Development: The Field;* and *Techniques for Effective Communication.* He served as President of the Academy of Human Resource Development (1993), the International Communication Association (1971), and the Western States Communication Association (1978). He also has received numerous awards for excellence and outstanding performance from both universities and professional associations.

Dr. Pace has consulted with and conducted management development activities with dozens of agencies and companies ranging from the Siemens Corporation, the South Australia Ambulance Service, the US Forest Service, Christensen Brothers Diamond Products, the Parks Sportsman company, the US Food Safety and Inspection Service, and the Parker Hannifin Corporation. He enjoys playing with his 20-plus grandchildren, climbing the rocks on the volcanic cliffs in Utah, and noncompetitive golf, Chinese Checkers, Birrguu Matya (an Australian Aboriginal game like Tic-Tac-Toe and Chess), Carpet Bowls, Nine Men Morris and lawn bowling (especially during the World Senior Games in St. George, Utah). He can be reached at <wpace@infowest.com>.

Index

I

Intuition and Inspiration Approach, 62, 66, 141
IRS, 100

J

Jewish, 126
John Hopkins Children Center, 113
Judaism, 126

K

Kiwanis, 51
Koestler, Arthur, 61
Kung Fu, 149

L

La Quebrada, 107
Lao-Tzu, 133
Leisure and Mental Health Conference, 111
Lincoln, Abraham, 136
Lions (club), 51
love, 2, 46, 128, 129

M

Malone, John, 10
marketers, 50

Maryland, 113
Matsumoto's, 73
Mexico, 107, 152
Mission Bay seminar, 113
Mission Bay, 82
Mohammed Ali, 46
monks, 134
Movers, 46, 47
mushin, 149, 152
Native Americans, 126
New Age, 126
No. 1 priority, 87
Nobel prize, 68, 128
Norman, Bix, 19

O

Oahu, Hawaii, 73
Operating Styles Profile, 45
organizational consultants, 24
Osborn, Alex F., 71

P

Parnes, Sydney, 61
Physical Wellness Test, 89
power, 34, 37, 48, 49, 98, 99, 101, 111, 117, 119, 125, 126, 129, 144, 150, 156
prioritize, 78, 85
problem solving, 51, 57, 59, 62, 69, 155
problem solving fallacy, 59
Probus, 51
Proverbs, 113, 118

University of Chicago, 111
University of Michigan, 129
USA Today, 27
Utah, 3, 111, 155-157

V

values, 88, 101, 102, 104, 105, 127, 128, 136, 142
Vivekananda, 119

W-Z

wellness, 89
Wilderotter, Maggie, 8
Zen riddle, 151, 152
Zen, 134, 151, 152
"zip your lip," 118, 120, 129, 145